The Process, The Promise

A journal for infertility prayer

LISHA EPPERSON

for my favorite lady, my mother - Mary Gh'Rael

Table of Contents

Preface.. vi

Dear Friend: On Prayer 1

How to Process the Lie of Why 4

Why You Have to Move Forward 6

When It's You.. 9

When It's Him… 14

Anger... 17

Day Off: Beautifully Made 20

Will Your Marriage Survive? 24

Why You Should Let Them In............................ 27

Faith, Science, Fertility…The Remix 30

Infertility and the Ordinary Girl....................... 36

Why You Should Feel Free to Grieve................ 40

Day Off: Feeling Fabulous................................ 42

My Best Friend's Pregnancy: The Other Side ... 44

I Choose Life - I.V.F. (I Vow Fertility) 47

Can You Forgive Betrayal? Can You Make Peace With Your Body During Infertility? 51

Do You Have a Plan?... 56

Walking by Faith.. 60

The Infertile Stepmother 65

Day Off: Love 68

Miscarriage 71

Watch Your Words...75

For The Day You Curse God...78

The Shift 80

How Will Motherhood Find You?.......................................82

What to Expect When You're Expecting after Infertility..............85

Have You Chosen to Be Still? Have You Found Yourself
Living Child-free? 88

When You Face the End of Your Fertility Journey.......................92

Day Off: Celebrating Transitions 95

When You Think Infertility is Forever: Tell Your Story 97

How to Thrive..100

Warrior Song 105

National Infertility Awareness Week 107

Acknowledgements 110

About the Author...112

Preface

Last fall I hopped on the bandwagon and opted in for **The Nester's 31 Day Writing Challenge**. Successfully blogging on one topic for a month seemed to be the ultimate stamp of certification for any online writer. Could I do it? My Twitter feed and Facebook page ran a continual stream of "I'm doing the challenge" posts from nearly everyone I knew …especially all my newbie blogger friends who had jumped on board.

At the last minute I decided to commit. It would be fun, right? My task was easy – pick a topic and write every day for 31 days, more or less. Easy enough instructions to follow.

I began my 31 day blog series with an arrow shooting straight at the heart of infertility. This was my topic. The Lord had used infertility to break me in the most beautiful way. I scratched out an outline in the notes section of my iPad and got to work.

By day nineteen I'd stretched myself beyond what I thought I could bare. I got very few comments, but people were reading. I prayerfully pushed forward.

By the time I reached Greenville, South Carolina for the Allume conference I'd hit my stride…I began to feel the elusive but powerful second wind. I had fresh eyes and a renewed heart for the topic. Still, when asked I'd bow low and mumble that I was writing about "infertility". I carried the shame of the word even as a writer. But God worked in me during the days I spent there and kept his promise throughout the process.

This book is the compilation of those posts. I share a literal flashback of my reproductive journey in hopes that you will begin thinking and talking about your own. I call it a lyrical journal of stories, prayers, and biblical truth. I've added a few questions for you and provided space for reflection. From "when it's you" facing infertility to the first flashes of menopause and late life motherhood...I wanted to create a safe place to ponder it all.

Thank you for reading and sharing
The Process, The Promise :: a journal for infertility prayer

Dear Friend: On Prayer

Be cheerful no matter what; pray all the time; thank God no matter what happens. This is the way God wants you who belong to Christ Jesus to live. **- 1 Thessalonians 5:16-18 The Message**

"Why must people kneel down to pray? If I really wanted to pray I'll tell you what I'd do. I'd go out into a great big field all alone or in the deep, deep woods and I'd look up into the sky—up— up—up—into that lovely blue sky that looks as if there was no end to its blueness. And then I'd just feel a prayer."
- L.M. Montgomery, Anne of Green Gables

As I mull over ideas and word, letting my thoughts flow freely, prayer begins.

Lord, help me. Jesus, Jesus, Jesus. Lord, I know. Each three word prayer, a conversation starter, opening the door for the real work of worship to begin. Offering His heart as a platform for whatever I have to say – He lets me talk. Then pours His best in spirit, leaving me speechless.

This is a prayer life. It's constant. A fluid exchange. A recycling of ideas between your head and heart given life by the giver of life. Every connection, a consecration and invocation. A divine intercession and expression.

A season of infertility is hard. Our prayers will sustain us. We offer them as holy sacrament to the Son who saves. We ground ourselves in this correspondence, this prayer dance and whimsical repartee. This is our love language. It's a holy litany and evensong. Our hearts breaking, for His.

I once thought prayers should follow a format. I made every effort to script the dialogue just right. Each word a step in the dance that leads to what we all want…the applause of an answer. It wasn't long before I gave up though and gave in to the simplicity, the lovely improvisational conversations that ensued, once I stopped trying.

Now? I sing "Whom have I in heaven but You?" He holds my secrets, shares my joy, keeps me laughing. I know he'll do the same for you. He'll cradle your heart, lift your spirit, commiserate with you over the stuff that hurts. All of it. He never misses a beat with what makes you laugh. He'll give you the words. He'll pour out, anoint, bless and change your perspective. I hope He never stops talking. I hope we never stop…listening.

These days, I don't blink an eye without recording it in my heart as evidence of grace poured over me. Another spiritual nod to the power I see working around me. And so it has become prayer - all of it - a whisper for help, an expression of gratitude, my love song, my devotion.

And God hears. Yes, God hears.

Following God's direction to pray through infertility may prove challenging but I think it's worthy of contemplation. Although I've experienced this walk, I've never walked it in your shoes. And "pain is personal", as Pastor Levi Lusko says. I listened to him preach online at the Skull Church with my son recently and later learned of the loss of his five year old daughter. He shared the reality of his family's pain in a raw and transparent post on his website. "It is impossible to feel anything except for what you are going through," he lamented. His words shot through my heart as I tossed around the idea of birthing these prayers here with you.

Infertility for you will be different than it has been for me – infertility will come to you as a unique set of experiences and expectations shaped by the now of your life. I honor your journey. My prayer though, is that you will be encouraged knowing you never walk alone in your struggle. My prayers are offered as a cry to heaven on your behalf, an offering brought before the throne in full acknowledgement that redemption comes from God alone.

But women, His warrior women pray. Know that women all over the world are praying - even for you.

How to Process the Lie of Why

"There are no "ifs" in God's world. And no places that are safer than other places. The center of His will is our only safety – let us pray that we may always know it." – **Corrie ten Boom**

Why? Women facing infertility want to know why. Some say it comes as a lesson, a lack of faith, a punishment, a curse - the result of a sin-fallen world? This side of heaven you'll probably never know. But what you can know is this - Gods' love. And if you can find your answer in God's love, well I'd go with that.

I hear the Deceiver tell it like this:

"Let's keep her focused on the question of "why?" She'll get lost in it and never see the cloak of love He's prepared. She'll run around in circles for years on that one."

"Yes! Let's wrap her in a web of lies. Tell her she's ugly, defective, a failure. Let's keep her eyes fixed and focused on the baby. She won't fulfill any of His will for her life. Yes. Let's keep her eyes on the baby."

But the Word says this...

"For I know the plans I have for you," says the Lord. "They are plans for good and not for disaster, to give you a future and a hope." **(Jeremiah 29:11)**

No, despite all these things, overwhelming victory is ours through Christ, who loved us.

"And I am convinced that nothing can ever separate us from God's love. Neither death nor life, neither angels nor demons, neither our fears for today nor our worries about tomorrow—not even the powers of hell can separate us from God's love. No power in the sky above or in the earth below—indeed, nothing in all creation will ever be able to separate us from the love of God that is revealed in Christ Jesus our Lord." **(Romans 8:37-39)**

Here's the truth about the lie. The lie is the opposite of love. If we focus on why, we lose. If we focus on the baby, we lose. "Why me" and "the baby" keep us in a lonely pool of confusion. We're left with an unanswered question and the worship of an idol. It leaves us vulnerable and open to an onslaught of deception.

We have to choose faith. Faith in God's love. Despite the trials we face, we must find our way back to the center.

The Prayer...

Lord open my eyes to your perfect truth. Deliver me from facts. My struggle is real, but I don't want to get lost. I don't want to miss You. Remind me to use Your word as a shield against lies. I receive Your truth, Your word, Your love. Amen.

For Reflection...

Are you stuck here? Has the lie of "why?" found you cycling in a pool of self-pity? Consider ways you can move forward by accepting that you may never know the answer. How can you live in contentment while you wait for His will concerning this area of your life?

Why You Have to Move Forward

"Go back?" he thought. "No good at all! Go sideways?
Impossible! Go forward? Only thing to do. On we go!"
– J.R.R. Tolkien, The Hobbit

You get a year. One year before your doctor recommends beginning some form of testing or treatment. And that's if you're under thirty-five. You get six months if you're older or if you've had other reproductive issues. The clock, every clock is always ticking.

Some shift immediately to overdrive - propelled to action.... they're fixers. But today I'm thinking about those who freeze. When facing uncharted waters and the uncertainty of the unknown the subtle, almost imperceptible movement of the clock lulls them to sleep. They're left complacent and unable to move forward. Is that you?

An infertility diagnosis is difficult to accept. Instead of relaxing into a new marriage, or simply feeling stress free about family planning - we don't and we can't. When we find ourselves on the road to motherhood, in many ways, a huge part of our life begins. We finally get to unwrap the childhood dream of motherhood. It's crushing when things don't go as planned or when the dream is taken away.

Motherhood is devalued. Society tells us there is so much more we can and should be. But the hint of an infertility issue awakens that primal desire; it's God-given, innate. Infertility is unacceptable when motherhood is who we are.

What's the next step? What happens when intuition tells you the doctor's right and there is a problem?

One step at a time. One day at a time.

Infertility is particularly hard for Christian women. We're trained to claim victory in every situation, to walk in healing and divine favor in every circumstance. This is essentially a good thing. But not when it pushes us into denial, and we can't see our way forward.

Don't let your faith push you into a season of passiveness. To be clear: there is a time and place for waiting on God. Stillness is a beautiful thing, but it's not to be confused with falling into a spiritual coma. We have to hear and obey God. You'll have peace if you've been instructed to sit still. If not, in obedience, actively pursue your faith.

Take steps. One day at a time. Don't fear, resist anxiety, but please move. Make the hard choices that never lead to regret.

The Word...

"If you listen obediently to the Voice of God, your God, and heartily obey all his commandments that I command you today, God, your God, will place you on high, high above all the nations of the world. All these blessings will come down on you and spread out beyond you because you have responded to the Voice of God, your God: God's blessing inside the city, God 's blessing in the country; God's blessing on your children, the crops of your land, the young of your livestock, the calves of your herds, the lambs of your flocks. God's blessing on your basket and bread bowl; God's blessing in your coming in, God's blessing in your going out." **(Deuteronomy 28:1-6, MSG)**

And a little inspiration to take that first step, (after hearing from God of course)

"She decided to start living the life she imagined." - **Kobi Yamada**

The Prayer...

Lord, I'm scared. I always thought I'd get pregnant when I felt ready. Guide my steps, give me wisdom as I make decisions about treatment and doctors. Free me from the fear that leads to missed opportunities and broken dreams. I have to hear your voice. Lead me as I actively seek your will. Amen.

For Reflection...

Have you been in the same spot for too long? Have you settled into a season of inactivity because of fear? Check in with yourself – do you have peace about that?

When It's You...

"Shame is the intensely painful feeling that we are unworthy of love and belonging." – **Brene Brown**

She walked in the privilege of health. Years of faithful service solidified confidence in her body's ability to pretty much respond, on command. So why was this different? The inner work and unseen moon magic of her body, its monthly systematic functioning was a given. Like clockwork. Predictable. On time. Dependable. But this was different.

She felt out of control. Powerless. Juicing. Yoga. Fasting. Herbs. Intentional relaxation. A vacation. Nothing seemed to work. This time her body would not perform. Her body would not respond to her commands for conception.

Hers is one of many versions of the same story – maybe it's yours. Whether it's fibroid tumors, endometriosis, polycystic ovarian disease, auto-immune disorders or previous life threatening illness, any of these ailments can lead you down a path of unanswered questions.

However you got here, the endless poking and prodding have revealed the problem and it's you. Forget all the male swagger about virility and sowing seed. Women who cannot physically bear children suffer a deep blow to their self-esteem. They scratch, claw and fight for the opportunity to give birth and will do almost anything to make it happen. When it's you - it hurts. When it's you, you feel shame.

You've been hit at your core and nothing makes sense. Every relationship is affected by this new challenge. Your friends and family can't possibly understand and your husband is afraid. He's not sure he can fix this. The career you've worked so hard to build feels pointless. Your concept of God has been shaken. You teeter between the familiar and unknown, wondering if you'll recover, if you'll ever feel a stabilizing, soul connecting foundation of faith beneath your feet again.

When it's you, you'll wonder if you're beautiful. You'll feel flawed. Defective. Broken. You'll wonder if he still loves you. Which takes us back to the lies: friend, don't believe it. If you believe the lie, you lose. Everything.

Cover yourself in God's beautifully and wonderfully made cloak of love. Remind yourself of His great plans for you. (He really does have plans for your life that have nothing to do with whether or not you ever give birth to a baby.) Set your heart to hope and rest... knowing your story isn't over.

Bishop T.D. Jakes makes it plain (and I'll paraphrase): "if the same problem from last year is holding you back this year, you're in containment." Check yourself - does this apply to you? Don't let infertility negatively define who you are or the woman God has called you to be.

If you've given your life to Him - you are in the center of His will. He is building and shaping your life's monument. It may be painful, but it is the deep chiseling that's necessary to refine a masterpiece. He loves you. Let Him complete the work.

The Word...

"For you created my inmost being; you knit me together in my mother's womb. I praise you because I am fearfully and wonderfully made; your works are wonderful; I know that full well." **(Psalm 139:13-14)**

The Prayer...

Lord, I didn't expect this. Infertility, my infertility, makes me feel ugly, broken. Your word says I'm fearfully and wonderfully made. My soul knows this well. But I don't feel it. Lord, help me define myself by your standards...your word. Free me from my emotions. Build me up in your truth. Amen.

For Reflection...

Does the infertility diagnosis find you at its core? It's not your fault. Do what you can with regard to treatment but do not blame yourself.

A Story...

My body didn't flower. No store-bought roses, no field picked flowers, not even my favorite hothouse peonies could bring hope to the deadness of my steel-gray, and shut womb. And I felt it. From my core, it traveled to every organ, decreasing flow, dimming signs of life, making me, less than vital. I tried to avoid a total shutdown by protecting my head, my heart. I didn't bloom.

I looked the part. I gained weight. My former dancer's body, no longer bound by years at the barre, filled out after a long denied freedom. Suddenly breasts, rounded hips and a belly protruded, but inside me was only the nothingness of my own dull pink, half-beating heart.

I liked my new body -thought it maternal, earthy. I imagined it preparing itself to receive life after years of working around the reality of a fibroid-filled uterus. Lifting and turning its rusty-brown soil with surgeries and procedures to make all things new. To receive a planting. To harvest. To bloom.

I found babies in soil - not my own,

a different garden - not of my planting.

In a golden field of God's goodness, he asked me to barter.

Trade my dream for His.

Springing forth flowers of a blessed bouquet, a pop-rock explosion and all manner of cosmic collisions leading me to the holy love of a child.

The petal soft lavender love of a child – it blew me away.

Love blew me away.

Love swept me away in a whirl wind of Cocoa Puff kisses and nighttime loving.

Jesus loved me good and back to life.

He set my soul ablaze with Holy Spirit fire. Illuminating flaming orange embers that would not. go. out. My joy was palpable. Unspeakable.

He gave me three beautiful reasons to let go of my blues. He pruned and plucked dead roots, over turned the soil of a forgotten wasteland.

Restored the broken, redeemed my hopeless. Jesus. Fixed. Me.

The barren dry landscape of a womb turned red.

Pulsing. Bleeding the holy water of life and every day working.

It's systematic functioning never ceased.

Because. The body believes. Because the body believes in life.

12

My body, given time, might bloom.

Can you feel the clear colors? Grays, pinks, browns, greens, yellows, blues - red? I felt each brush stroke.

The mixing and choosing of colors hurt – a violent blending, a hopeful ending.

Waiting for the paint to dry takes time. His art came to life in mine.

"Every flower is a soul blossoming in nature." - **Gérard de Nerval**

It's not your fault. Receive that.

When It's Him...

"Have enough courage to trust love one more time and always one more time." – **Maya Angelou**

My infertility story cast me in the starring role. It was me. But I wondered how I would handle infertility if the roles were reversed - if I had to deal with my husband's infertility? We all speak the honorable words people expect to hear: "I love you honey, it doesn't matter." But my heart wasn't so pure. I wondered how I'd handle male factor infertility. When it's your husband, what do you do?

Visions of pregnancy don't lead men to marriage. Before we're seen as mothers, they think of us as lovers. It's different for women. We're attracted to the vision of men as fathers. We imagine becoming the mothers of our husbands' children. We imagine our bellies full of promise, and that dream begins, when we imagine being a wife. When it's him, you'll have to be careful. Not only are you grieving the loss of potential biological children together, you are handling the ego of a man who finds himself unable to provide an heir, a genetic link to the future. His identity is tied to being a good provider *and* a great lover. Let's be real ladies, being told or teased that he's shooting blanks or doesn't know how to "do it" won't go over well.

And what of you? Will you view him differently? Will you blame him? Will you emotionally walk away from your marriage? For him, infertility is emasculating. He wants to be your powerful lover but sees himself as a failure. A fundamental part of his identity is tied to being able to take care of you (this includes getting you pregnant, meeting your needs). When he can't, he needs time to process.

I often imagined connecting with my best male buddies in a round table of truth about fertility. I'd confront them with this question: Would you see your wife differently if she couldn't bear children? Would it be a deal breaker?

Historically it was. If your husband couldn't produce a child, his brother would step in. If you couldn't, he'd be free to step outside the marriage to produce an heir. Thank God we live in a time where infertility is medically recognized as a disease, but it takes a lot longer to change the thought patterns of an entire society. Voices that scream infertility is a generational curse, the heavy price we pay for something somebody, somewhere did wrong, are loud and carry far. Infertility is no one's fault, but humans feel most comfortable assigning blame. Somebody is at fault, and when it's your husband it's hard.

When it's him, you'll have to check your heart, making sure old ideas and patterns of thinking aren't clouding your view. You'll have to tenderly nurture your wounds while caring for his broken heart. Bruises come easily and the wrong words are almost impossible to retract. Be careful.

Male factor infertility is rarely talked about, and its emotional toll on men is grossly overlooked. Men who struggle in this area have limited resources and there are few safe places for them to share their burdens. That's where you come in, as gate-keeper for the marriage you cherish. Have courage. Stay prayerful.

The Word...

"Bear one another's burdens, and so fulfill the law of Christ." **(Galatians 6:2)**

"Therefore shall a man leave his father and his mother and shall cleave unto his wife and the two shall be one flesh." **(Genesis 2:24 KJV)**

The Prayer...

Lord, we're hurting. My beautiful husband is hurting and I can't fix it. Help me to gently minister your love. Remove blame, shame, and denial. Draw us closer together. Even in this. Amen.

For Reflection...

It's not his fault. Tell him you don't blame him. Love on him the way you would if it were your best friend. Because guess what? It is.

Anger

I'm angry

I feel the piping hot kettle rage of an explosion in the making

Rivers of angry hot tears singe holes in my heart

I'm tired and it's hard to breathe

There are no answers

Nothing I can do to right this wrong

Bring calm to the crazy of this storm

I'm angry

I feel the ebb of transition

Creeping slowly -...- change is coming

My anger has reached its peak

It must transform or die, morph or expire

So it's time to choose

Exist as love or hate?

The time is NOW

To choose good, to expect God

I'll sit here

And wait....

Slowly gather my thoughts

Open the door, let His revolution begin

Let the blessing of love take over

Carry me

Let the waves and rhythm of His eternal essence

Carry me to the other side

Yes, I'm Alive

There's life in my anger

This holy, righteous rage

Propels faith into action

To move forward, up and out of this sorrowful pit

I'll make choices, confront the hard things

Take steps towards my destiny

My future is bright

I'll look back someday

And give thanks -...- for the expression -...- of my God-
sanctioned anger

The Word...

"Be angry, and yet do not sin; do not let the sun go down on
your anger, and do not give the devil an opportunity."
(Ephesians 4: 26-27)

"But let patience have her perfect work, that ye may be perfect
and entire, wanting nothing." **(James 1:4)**

The Prayer...

Lord, I'm angry. Help me to propel this righteous anger into active faith. Help me confront the hard things. Grace me to be a warrior, confident my strength is found in You. Amen.

For Reflection...

Are you angry? Has it turned to bitterness? Give Him your whole heart on this one. Forgive by releasing the burden you've placed on yourself. Take some time to explore your feelings by writing them down.

Day Off: Beautifully Made

"Think of all the beauty still left around you and be happy."

— Anne Frank

One of the most important things you can do during your infertility journey is learn to take time off. Whether you plan a lunch date with a friend or take a dance class followed by a healthy dose of window shopping, learn to nurture the girl inside with what I call a "mental health holiday." God gives us permission to rest. Rest revives. We see more clearly and awake with fresh perspective. We re-emerge - hopeful. You need a day off.

Day off

Rest, happy tears, peace, solitude, play, chocolate, singing, quiet time, joy, hugs

Day off

Shopping, friends, love, laughter, dancing, naptime, nothing, a good book, coffee... anything.

Thank you Lord for a day off

So laying aside our troubles, let's strive to explore our creative individuality. Let's celebrate the beautifully made - YOU.

What or who energizes you creatively? Let me introduce you to two women who motivate me to put my best foot forward. They share a commitment to creativity that screams "Life...is for living!"

Debbie Hardy realized her dream for a fashion house. It's called Martine's' Dream. There, you'll find whimsical, colorful creations inspired by India and her love for the sun. Long, sheer, flowing - perfect for a mid-year island vacation or weekend getaway with the girls. I wear mine all summer and then make myself happy lounging around the house in beautiful prints all winter. I don't know anyone who doesn't feel a foot taller and all the more lovely in anything she creates.

Patsy Paterno was number forty-three at The Nesters' 31 Day Writing challenge in 2014. I've been quietly inspired by her work and lurk around her blog to soak up the beauty. Take a look at her lovely prints with praise at HeArtWorks. Everything looks like it was created in an underwater paradise. Think aquatic, think the word, think women, think color – all coming together in a sea of pretty. I love it.

The expression, beauty, and power of dance makes me want to fly. Something about pushing the human form physically, challenging the body to act out grace lifts my spirit. From the exquisite perfection of companies like Alvin Ailey to street dancers turning it out on a subway platform, I'm always intrigued, always moved. I believe dance, all art really, heals both the audience and the performer. You don't have to be a professional to offer worship like this. Push back the sofa, press play on your favorite song and allow Him to have His way in your temple. It's personal and private, and there is no right or wrong. So be free to give it everything you've got.

For dancing inspiration...

Check out Clarissa S. Stroud

Dancing to "You Amaze Me" by Vicky Yohe

http://youtu.be/JsAiF-EnjGA

The Word...

"God, my shepherd! I don't need a thing. You have bedded me down in lush meadows, you find me quiet pools to drink from. True to your word, you let me catch my breath and send me in the right direction." - **(Psalm 23:1-3, MSG)**

For Reflection...

Beautiful.

Lovely, gorgeous, stunning.

On the surface it's about physical appearance.

But the first fragile layer cracks easily.

It is fallow ground meant to be broken.

Push past it to reveal a rock solid core, covered with a gritty sheet of blood and bone.

Beautiful is not always pretty.

Beautiful.

Some beauty is God-given, some earned.

A tear-stained face, a battle cry, and finally, maybe a victory dance?

Whether or not she won is of little importance.

She is beautiful not because of the win but because of the work.

My soul acknowledges the work and knows the deeper meaning of this word.

Beautiful is holy and dirty.

Beautiful is graceful and chaotic.

Beautiful is the tingly thrill of laughter and so much pain.

Beautiful is unimagined strength. Beautiful is work.

Beautiful.

Don't be fooled by the fluid lines of a dancer as she seamlessly flows from one movement to the next. Much of the work is done behind the scenes – the unseen labor of the in-between. You can't explain how she transitioned from one position to another. She arrives and you experience the beauty of NOW.

That - is beautiful.

Beautiful.

Beautiful isn't always easy. It is diligence. Beautiful is focus.

The pursuit of a dream is beautiful.

Shrouded in the veil of purpose, we are beautiful.

Pushed to our self-imposed limits - the next step is beautiful. Because you took it when you thought you couldn't, you, are beautiful.

Beautiful.

You are beautiful when you try.

No matter the outcome of your efforts.

It was never the win - it was the work.

Your work was beautiful.

I'd love to hear about something you lovingly labored over, poured sweat to carry out. Let's take a moment to think about your beautiful.

No questions today…Go. Do. Be.

Will Your Marriage Survive?

Did infertility show up at your wedding? An uninvited guest squeezing her way onto the dance floor, she may have crept in unnoticed. She wasn't invited but she's determined to undermine the hard work and time invested in your union. Through disappointment and distraction, she'll work to destroy one or both of you.

Many couples don't make it. They crumble under the weight of this unexpected pressure. When your love life's a public hot topic, it's easy to feel like a failure. Constant questions and insensitive comments create stress and leave scars. On display and without the goods, your union can feel like a mistake. Will your marriage survive?

Who wants to be that couple? The universal message? Fertility is sexy, attractive, a sign of prosperity. So how do you keep it hot and heavy when your quiver isn't full? Sex feels unproductive and well, unsexy. Timing, temperatures and tantrums. It's hot in your bedroom, but for all the wrong reasons. Once passionate dialogue eventually turns cold. It becomes easier not to talk.

How can you keep your marriage alive? How can you stay friends? Is it possible for a marriage to thrive when faced with infertility? Will your marriage survive?

Here's the hope ...Communication. Loving confrontation and laughter. The couples who communicate successfully pass the test. They stay on the same team. They've learned to speak each other's language and communicate in the millions of little ways that keep love alive. The successful couples let friends in, but know when to keep them out. They face trials together. They do the hard thing and stay focused. They still look each other in the eye. When it matters, they call each other out rather than let things slide. They laugh. They create a culture of love that includes making each other smile. Daily. They forgive. Daily. The couples that survive remain hopeful and make decisions together. They cry. They believe God. They come out stronger. United. Beautifully bound. Inextricably woven. No matter the outcome, these couples win!

The Word...

"Though one may be overpowered, two can defend themselves. A cord of three strands is not quickly broken." **(Ecclesiastes 4:12)**

The Prayer...

Lord, because of your love, we can face any trial. We can emerge triumphant. We acknowledge you as the final authority over our marriage and surrender our emotions and desires. We have each other. We have You. Help us take care of each other in service and honor to our union. Bless our communication. Give us reasons to laugh and reasons to remain hopeful. Our marriage is a gift. We thank you for it. Amen.

For Reflection....

Infertility is a shared journey. Despite who receives the diagnosis, you're in this together. So...

Spend time together. Infertility has a way of pushing us to our separate corners. Men and women process feelings differently and that difference however subtle can keep us apart. So...

Plan a date - talk about anything but infertility. Remember how funny he is, let him make you laugh. He loves to see you smile.

Plan a date - talk about infertility. Discuss your most recent treatment plan. Are you feeling optimistic? Doubtful? Make plans for your next step.

Being intimate, only during your fertile time is a joy stealer and puts too much pressure on what should be a relationship builder. Keep covenant with your husband by honoring spontaneity.

Pick a prayer night - express your fears and concerns. Be transparent about your feelings of hopelessness. Listen. Encourage each other. Be willing to bear the burden when he's having a particularly doubtful day...allow him to do the same for you.

Plan a vacation and buy yourself something fabulous to wear, but don't factor in whether or not you'll be pregnant. Go because you want to and buy it because it's beautiful on your body, now.

Remember to laugh. Infertility isn't funny, but it's important to find humor.

Why You Should Let Them In

Your parents understand in a way no one else will. Your friends love you and really do want to see you happy. God is not punishing you.

When we're hurting, it's easy to shut people out - those closest to us and God. He's allowing this. By some crazy defect in His decision making process, He's allowing you to suffer. How can you connect with Him?

We have to learn to let them in. Our tendency to isolate leaves us vulnerable. Like wounded puppies, we retreat to a corner to take care of ourselves. Problem is - we aren't designed like that. We were created for connection. We crave community and thrive on our ability to engage one with another. We need each other.

I know. No one wants to say they need anyone or anything anymore. But we do. When faced with infertility, you do.

True, people say insensitive things. But they don't mean them, and if we don't engage in relationship, they'll never know their words hurt. They won't understand. They'll repeat them. The cycle continues, and that's sad. Because it doesn't have to be this way. We have a responsibility to each other to offer support through the hard stuff. We have a responsibility to experience each side: as encourager and as one who needs encouragement. In this way, we engage in the beautifully organic reciprocity of community. If we let it, this could heal us. It could create the kind of paradigm shift whereby love infiltrates the cracks in our community. Healing could be real.

But we have to let them in.

Here's the promise: in community we find God. His hands and heart are made available to us on earth through relationship. Our friendships refine, undergird and increase us. Our friendships free us from the secrecy of silence. When we let them in, friends validate the truth. They are the witnesses who hold our stories. We can't hold them alone.

We'll have to open the door.

When we open the door we receive prayer. We get a shoulder to cry on, someone to laugh with. Opening the door presents opportunities for grace. We hear and are heard. You won't regret opening the door. When you share your story, you'll hear whispers of warriors all over the world as they cry out "me too." Those powerful, grace-filled moments of shared experience assure us of His presence. We are not alone.

I didn't always get this right. The pain of infertility often promotes a cycle of silence; even people going through it don't reach out to each other. That's changing, and that's good.

Maybe you don't want your friends to know, maybe you're embarrassed, but today - there is no reason you can't have a cushion of community to love you through a hard season. You don't have to and you shouldn't suffer alone.

The Prayer...

Lord I need community. Help me open the door. Free me from a cycle of silence that leaves me vulnerable - an easy target for doubt and unbelief. Use my relationships as your hands and heart, your tangible love here on earth. I receive the blessing of friendship. Amen.

Inspiration…

"A faithful friend is a strong defense; And he that hath found him hath found a treasure." - **Louisa May Alcott**

"There is no greater agony than bearing an untold story inside you." - **Maya Angelou**

The Word…

"The heartfelt counsel of a friend is as sweet as perfume and incense." (**Proverbs 27:9**)

"As iron sharpens iron, so a friend sharpens a friend." (**Proverbs 27:17**)

To do…

Connect now - online or in real life. Connect.

A website for encouragement and community: **fertilethoughts.com**

A Facebook group to help you connect: **THRIVE(in)fertility**

Faith, Science, Fertility...The Remix

Questions about faith, science, and fertility left me alone and in the middle of the darkest part of the journey. What is infertility but a confounded mess of injustice - a relentless and underhanded foe? In the darkness, I blindly groped for truth. I struggled. I had to fight for the win. Infertility for the Christian woman is hard, and I questioned God every step of the way.

This is an area you'll have to conquer alone. Faith is like that. Your friends can believe for you, but the road is yours to travel. You'll have to figure out where the three collide: faith, science, and infertility. You'll have to reconcile your beliefs with the reality of a faith shattering experience. I wish I could do this for you - meld them together, make it all make sense. What I can do is share my story. Believing the redemptive expression of a story can play a significant role in healing, I share it openly.

Here's the hope - there is light at the end of the tunnel. The collision of your faith with anything can create a miracle. It's that powerful.

This is an important one friends. Breathe deeply. Get ready for the battle.

Faith. Science. Fertility. Three powerful words. Standing alone, each one seems clear. You have some idea what each means in your life, how it affects you. But together, they cloud your typically 20/20 vision. When trying to conceive, you're left standing alone with a cartoon bubble full of question marks over your head – all related to these words. How do you define them? How do you put them together to bring a quiet peace to an ever-searching heart? I am tearful as I write this because these three words have brought me the most significant challenge of my life, and I hope that by talking about it I can help someone else. I pray it is useful.

I gave my heart to God at twenty-three. The man I now call husband brought me to church as part of our courtship. My relationship with *him* developed as I got to know the greatest Him of all. Up until that point, I had never been acquainted with loss. Having grown up surrounded by parents, family, and friends who supported and loved me, I was living the blessed life. Sure, I had cried the crocodile tears of first love. I'd even felt my share of betrayal. But I had never known the soul-crushing pain I would experience as a newly married woman.

A year and a half into our marriage, I conceived and miscarried our first child. Fourteen weeks. No heartbeat. No life. Gone. I was devastated. My heart? Broken. Initially I martyred it off. Professing my wholeness after what was seemingly God's plan, I took two weeks off and then returned to life. I didn't know it at the time, but the experience had changed me forever. Slowly, over a period of months and years, I lost my faith and lived in unbelief. All of this closeted, though. I still attended, sang in, and served in church. I knew God was love. I just no longer believed He loved me. How could He and allow me to lose our baby? My faith was being tested.

This is where it gets tricky. I love science and have always had a whimsical curiosity about the wonders of the universe. At the same time, I never doubted God as creator of it all. In the same way, I respect the medical field, and I believe God gives wisdom to doctors to create treatment protocols and uses them as instruments of healing. Then why, when considering treatment for the disease of infertility, did I believe I wasn't exercising my faith if I sought advice from a doctor? This misguided information regarding barrenness is subtly passed among the pews of too many churches. It leaves a trail of confusion and guilt that God did not intend. I vacillated on this one for a long time and eventually felt led to see a doctor. I saw it as exercising my dust-mite sized faith with a corresponding action, though that initial fear, that *I* was the misguided one, still haunted me.

My journey down the path of medicine did not lead to a baby. I travelled the road as long as it felt comfortable and got off just a few short exits from my starting point. I was okay with it. Emotionally and physically I was tired, but I thank God I was able to get on and off the roller coaster of treatment at my choosing. I appreciated the doctors and nurses I met who acknowledged God in their efforts. Their approach was refreshing and gave me peace during a particularly vulnerable time.

Ultimately, time was a healer, and as the years went by, I regained my faith. I reached a crossroads in my walk with God where it was either *put up or shut up*. Most people get to this point eventually. Something happens that rocks your core, you have to pick up your cross and keep it moving or walk away - empty handed and full of pride.

"Why can't I, why won't you?" "Crack addicts have babies! Why not me?" This is a sampling of the stream of internal dialogue I had with God. I was angry with Him. I did not like Him. His love seemed cruel and unkind and I wanted no part of it. I'm sure somewhere in the heavens a door slammed every time I ran off to my room crying. I was mad. But time healed me, and I grew up in the things of God. I made my choice and decided that baby or no baby, I was in this thing for good. I began to listen for, hear, and obey His voice. He called me to the ministry of adoption and I answered yes. I became a mother and got a glimpse of life He'd planned and set aside just for me.

By the time I conceived my only biological child I was forty-four years old. Everything the doctors had said was a problem, plagued me still. But God said yes. By the time my son was conceived, I had begun to want to believe for a miracle again. The teaching I was receiving lit a fire in me that made me want to have this thing I had long since put on the shelf. I sowed for him, I prayed for him. But I really don't remember the stress of all that. I had found the peace I'd searched for. Whether I ever achieved a full-term pregnancy and healthy baby had already been dealt with. I had made peace with God.

I know intimately the pain of infertility and to this day wear proudly, the scars it left behind. I know I survived and I know God is using my experience to His glory. However, I could never tell a fellow fertility warrior that she doesn't have a baby because her faith isn't strong enough. That is just not a call I'm qualified to make. Only God knows and sees the heart of His creation.

But I urge you to believe God. He is a miracle-working God and He can work a miracle in your situation. For me, the miracles began with the adoption of my first spirit baby. At the time, I thought I had reached the summit - reached the high note of my life. I thought I could go no higher and get no happier, but there was so much more. So believe Him. Not solely because you think there is a biological child at the end of the road, but just because you believe Him - whatever the plan for your life may be. Because that's what faith is.

Praise God for science and the changes and growth in reproductive medicine that have allowed hundreds of thousands of women to become mothers. There is no condemnation in Christ and there should be no faith-bashing of women who are seeking treatment for a disease from a medical doctor. This also applies to women who seek treatment from naturopaths and herbalists. The reality of food as medicine is powerful, and we are wise when we carefully consider the connection between our diet and health. God meets each of us where we are, and there should be no judgment. Too many women have been fed the lie that seeking treatment is a lack of faith. When women believe the lies, they are allowing the enemy to slowly kill their dream of parenthood.

There's an addendum to that dreadful memo about fertility, and it pertains to adoption. No one says it, but many believers feel the adoption of a child would somehow nullify their faith walk. Let's be clear: if God calls you to motherhood and has given you a passion and desire for it, know that the call is yours. The details of how it will happen may not be clear, but please know that seeing a doctor or adopting a child are not automatic faith-busters. Even unbelievers tuck a prayer card in their pockets when visiting a doctor, and I can't begin to tell you about the faith required to consider the adoption process. In the end, it's all faith.

Faith. Science. Fertility. Faith, Science, Fertility. Faith. Science. Fertility. Faith....

The Word...

"Show me your ways, Lord, teach me your paths. Guide me in your truth and teach me, for you are God my Savior, and my hope is in you all day long." **(Psalm 25:4-5)**

The Prayer...

Lord, I trust you. Show me your way. Lead me as I walk in your truth. Guide each step. Every choice. More than anything, I want peace. More than anything, I want you. Make your will known. Amen.

For Reflection…

Are you in treatment and feeling guilty? Have you stalled treatment because you think God will punish you for not having enough faith? Do you feel called to adopt and have the same faith busting feelings?

God will give you the grace to find peace in your decisions. You already have enough faith. Go find your peace.

Infertility and the Ordinary Girl

You're no ordinary girl. Singled out when you'd prefer being like the others, you want to blend in. You're here, and you don't want to be. Forced to stand in line. You're here because you're different.

You can't make sense of this line. Who's next, you wonder? There's no first come, first served; it isn't organized alphabetically. You've seen women jump ahead of you from the back of the line. For no clear reason. Is it the perfect pale yellow of her blouse or does she have an in with the teacher? No. You've been pulled aside and asked to wait.

> You wanted to be like them - the ordinary women
> Their bodies, cycles, births - a hushed given
> They carelessly fall pregnant while you stand in line
> To learn a few lessons, pass a few tests in a school for the broken

Hopefully your time will be short. Prayerfully you'll learn a few things: there's grace, compassion - gratitude. You'll be tried beyond what you think you can stand. You will undoubtedly question your identity - because infertility is nothing if not a breaker of wills, a killer of self-esteem. It will be hard. Waiting is hard and infertility isn't for ordinary girls.

I wanted to be like them. Make love to my husband. Get pregnant. Sounds simple enough. But you see, I'm like you - I wasn't ordinary either.

> I had an ordinary body that refused to do an ordinary thing
> Conception was normal and my body wouldn't do it.
> So while they planned baby showers and talked breast-feeding

I window-shopped or did yoga...anything to keep me from remembering. I wasn't like them. I wasn't ordinary.

And I wanted to be

I'd have given anything to be ordinary but I had to learn to embrace my own path, my *own*, common, run of the mill - ordinary. I had to restrict time spent glancing back at what others were doing because their ordinary wasn't mine. And coveting it only held me back from walking in a life that could be extra-ordinary. I learned we're all different - unique creations of an amazing God. We're all different, and who's to say the line was a bad thing anyway? *

What will you do while waiting? Will a good book pass the time? A few long overdue conversations with friends? I know this is hard to hear, but it's important, because the years pass and you don't want to take for granted the beautifully ordinary gift of life. You have to choose to keep living.

You can serve others by offering your gifts back to God. Sow your energy and time as a servant to your community. Because this time is special. As a woman without children, you are free in a way you'll never be again. It's up to us to draw out the advantages of the situations we find ourselves in - extract His goodness and enjoy every drop of the nectar of life.

Friends, we get to choose. Choice is a gift, an overlooked bit of ordinary grace extended to us because of love. We "get" to choose. Let's choose to thrive.

We can pass the time together - create our own club. We of the rare breed, the different cloth: we are warrior women. We can redeem the time by shouting down the walls. We may have to wait, but we haven't been silenced. Let us redeem the expression of our worth, creatively explore our callings. Let's tell our stories and in the telling be healed. Let's revive our hearts through communion with His spirit. Living this way makes *your* ordinary extraordinary.

Experiment with this for a few weeks. You'll find fulfillment. I promise.
So here's to being healthier and happier while waiting. How will you embrace *your* ordinary?

* I spent enough time on and off the line to say it produced compassion, faith and resilience. I wouldn't trade the experience. Other warriors say the same. Beauty was found in the brokenness...and remains...in my gorgeous ordinary.

The Word...

"I pray to God —my life a prayer— and wait for what he'll say and do. My life's on the line before God, my Lord, waiting and watching till morning, waiting and watching till morning." **(Psalm 130:5, 6 MSG)**

"So let's not allow ourselves to get fatigued doing good. At the right time we will harvest a good crop if we don't give up, or quit. Right now, therefore, every time we get the chance, let us work for the benefit of all, starting with the people closest to us in the community of faith." **(Galatians 6:9, 10 MSG)**

The Prayer...

Lord, help me wait on you. I want to wait with grace. I want to embrace and fully appreciate the gift of life. In this season of waiting, I want to be found serving, offering my talent and ability back to you. I want to redeem the expression of my worth, creatively explore my calling. You've graced me with a choice, and I choose life. Amen.

For Reflection…

What is your redemptive expression? How can you creatively serve the kingdom while waiting? Sign up for a club, verbally commit to being held accountable for service to others. While waiting meditate on savoring life – showing genuine gratitude. What would that look like?

Why You Should Feel Free to Grieve

I remember the day my heart broke. I felt it crack, break apart in a million little pieces. My heart could no longer hold the hurt. It wasn't meant to.

Four years of questions. Four years of faking it. The indescribable pain of loss. I was okay. Really. I wanted to count it all joy, pass the test, and stand strong in my faith. I couldn't cry. I refused to be broken. My heart was full of unspoken dreams. I clutched tightly to this private pain.

Then, I let go on the kitchen floor in our tiny railroad apartment. I cried. Tears rushed free in a flood that wouldn't, couldn't be stopped. Falling to my knees, my heart broke. Freedom was my reward for the breakthrough, freedom was the prize. It was a process, but I claimed it.

I began to talk about it. First to people on the fringes. Infrequent and generally unplanned interactions felt safe. I worked towards the inner circle, ending in full disclosure with my best friend. She knew of course, but I'd never said a word. Full of pride and not wanting to appear weak or out of control, I hid behind conversations focused on her. My story crept out slowly, in pieces much like the remnants of my heart. Reconstruction was a promise. I prayed for its fulfillment.

The complex emotions of infertility demand expression, an outlet for the grief we silently carry. It's hard to talk about something no one can see. The inner turmoil of our private yearning is not up for discussion. Classified as bedroom talk, we don't speak of such things publicly.

Give yourself permission to grieve. Your disappointment isn't selfish. Tears are cleansing, and you don't always have to put on a brave face. You were created human, a perfectly and beautifully flawed human. Designed for connection with God and man, you have a heart. It belongs to Him. Trust Him to heal it as you grieve.

Don't get lost in grief but feel free to have a good cry when you need to. Your sacred circle of family and friends will be there to catch you. They'll encourage and pick you up if you stay down too long.

Your emotional health is important. Make the powerful choice to take care of yourself. Get the help you need to process the emotions of infertility. Free yourself with the gift of tears. Feel free to grieve.

The Word...

"My life dissolves and weeps itself away for heaviness; raise me up and strengthen me according to [the promises of] Your word." **(Psalm 119:28 AMP)**

The Prayer...

Lord, I can't hold this anymore. This burden is too heavy. I have to lay it down. I have to grieve. I feel freedom rushing in, washing over me in waves of relief, a glorious release. Strengthen me in your word. I'm counting on your promise of restoration. Thank you for the assurance of your love. Amen.

For Reflection...

Have you given yourself permission to grieve? Do you have a safe space to share your feelings about infertility?

Day Off: Feeling Fabulous

I fell in love with head wraps when I started growing dreadlocks. Having worn my hair natural (no chemical relaxers) since my early twenties, I thought it would twist and twirl together instantly. I was wrong. The first year was a nightmare. My natural hair isn't curly. It has a very slight wave pattern and resembles stretched lamb's wool. It took a year for it to coil around itself permanently. By the third month, the baby twists I started with looked a mess.

Don't get me wrong; I appreciate the process. And if a rootsy, rock reggae look is what you're going for, do you. But I wanted a classically groomed look and I just didn't have it. I had to wait. Growing my hair was a beautiful lesson in patience. Each stage brought different challenges. Year one was by far the most difficult.

Wrapping my hair saved the day. I think every woman should have a head wrap in her stash of accessories. They instantly beautify and can be worn in any season. And most importantly, they gracefully disguise bad hair days. Head wraps are perfect for a day off. Mine is part of the **EPPERSON** collection. One piece, and super easy to style.

****

I may be late to the party, but I'm loving **Misty Edwards**. Worship leader, minister, cancer survivor. I love her clear strong voice. It confidently rests on top of the music. I hear her above it, if that makes sense. She's a Jesus lover with an earthy, puritan, grunge style. She's a "friend in my head."

The Word...

"When life is heavy and hard to take, go off by yourself. Enter the silence. Bow in prayer. Don't ask questions: Wait for hope to appear. Don't run from trouble. Take it full-face. The "worst" is never the worst." - **(Lamentations 3:28-30 MSG)**

The Prayer...

Lord, I'm feeling good today. I'm walking in your word and feeling your love. Thank you for ministering my worth, quietly whispering words of love - just when I need them. Your love is amazing. I am whole. I have peace. You are good. Amen.

For Reflection:

How do you fake the fabulous? What's your go to style when you can't pull it together but have to? Pull yourself together and take a picture. Share your tips with a friend.

My Best Friend's Pregnancy: The Other Side

Rose was pregnant again, expecting number three when Camille's body struggled to physically embrace even one. The life cycle as manifested through pregnancy had dealt a dirty hand, and the ordinary miracle of pregnancy remained, for Camille, a mystery. Of all the joys they could share, pregnancy was not one of them. It wasn't fair.

Best friend's, Rose knew about Camille's struggle, but couldn't contain her own excitement. A new baby *is* exciting and she couldn't pretend she wasn't thrilled to carry life again. Infertility was hard on their relationship. Pulling them apart, creating a bridge neither of them could cross. They were living in two different worlds.

The women gathered. They gathered in the hallway after church every Sunday. Only today, they spilled into the open space like so many children on a playground. The news had spread! Everyone knew what the envelope she clutched contained. Sure, there'd be hugs and plans for lunch. Service went long, and they were hungry. But the women gathered today to celebrate life. Rose would confirm her pregnancy by saying the words. She'd own her pregnancy with a bold declaration. Today, Rose would share her sonogram.

She didn't see Camille. Always the first to smile, always her shoulder to lean on, processor of opinions and fiercely loyal comrade, Camille was her best friend.

Today the women collected near the entrance of the children's ministry. Rose stood in the center, balancing the scan in her hands as an offering, palms outstretched. The women gathered and marveled at the picture. Nine weeks. She was nine weeks along and the ball of cells that would become a baby was beginning to look like one. Congratulations and hugs, sweet words and blessings enveloped her. Everyone was there except Camille.

Then she saw her, moving quickly through the crowd. Camille seemed an other worldly apparition, more angelic than human. In the blink of an eye, she dashed across the hallway and out the door. In a perfect world she would have paused, made eye contact. They would have leaped over the wall dividing them. But the world isn't perfect, and life isn't fair. In real-time she paused - but not long enough to grab hold of grace tearing at the edges of the crowd. She couldn't look at Rose. She ran.

But her presence was felt. Because Camille's was the hand she wanted to hold. Because their connection was more sister than friend. Because heart and soul had bonded over the years. This was spiritual. Rose felt a tingle up her spine and a pinch in her heart. Her hands parted. The sonogram fell to the floor.

Downstairs in her car, Camille barely opened the door before bursting into a hot rush of tears. It wasn't fair. It wasn't fair.

How do you happily embrace your best friend's pregnancy? When denied the very thing offered to her so freely, how do you plan and dream? How do you rejoice? Can you be authentically happy for her? How do you communicate when feeling isolated?

I want to tell both sides because it's hard for your friend who is pregnant too. It's a two-way dilemma. Infertility creates a wall you'll have to carefully climb together. There is no right way for her to tell you; no wrong way for you to respond. As the one going through infertility, you'll tend to shut others out. If we could hear their hearts, we'd know how important it is to stay connected. If you agree to love each other and hold onto God, you'll see your way through the maze. Love each other through the disappointment, the triumphs. It isn't easy but you can stay friends through infertility. You can meet in the middle and sometimes, truly rejoice.

The Word...

"Wherefore comfort yourselves together, and edify one another, even as also ye do." - **(1 Thessalonians 5:11)**

The Prayer...

Lord, we thank you for the bond of friendship and approach you as sisters. We are your daughters. We're in different seasons of life and want to remain close. Help us do that. Let our connection be sustained by your love. Help us to gracefully participate in each other's lives remaining sensitive to each heart. Help us recognize when you speak. Hearing above all else...your voice. Amen.

For Reflection...

Know that your friends will understand. If you don't attend the baby shower, if you don't immediately rush in to hold the baby, if you sometimes...have no words. Your friends understand. On the flip side, in your own way try to rejoice with her, even if it's a knowing glance, a greeting card, or letter - let her know you are happy for her.

I Choose Life - I.V.F. (I Vow Fertility)

Oh no, not I

I will survive

Oh as long as I know how to love

I know I'll stay alive

I've got all my life to live

I've got all my love to give

And I'll survive, I will survive (hey-hey) – **Gloria Gaynor**

People wonder and sometimes gather the courage to ask. What did you do? How did you get through it? Infertility was a huge chapter in the story of my life. Walking through it shaped a large part of who I am today. But I wanted the experience to be positive. I'm one of those the glass-is-half-full girls. Give me the lemons; I'll make fabulous lemonade.

So I'll share today how I did it. There was never a magic bullet, and I fully trust God's plans for us as individuals {keep that in mind, it's important.} What I do know is this: it all begins with a shift in focus; it starts with perspective. How do you see yourself and do you truly want to live?

Infertility attacks our sense of self-worth first. The central strategy of this battle is to destroy your life. What better way than an assault on your worth? A negative self-image keeps our lives stagnant. No motion. No growth. Lack of productivity. Infertile.

The biggest change for me occurred when I vowed fertility in life. I couldn't accept the current version of my life and refused to allow it to continue. I took control by making a choice. Any devastating life situation can knock us off track. Will you get back up? Will you be better? Bottom line...if you stay in the race (your race) - you win. The women who defeat barrenness vow fertility in life. They live life with intention and refuse the role of victim. They get back up.

Infertility doesn't have to win. Instead, vow fertility.

fer·til·i·ty - the quality of being fertile; productiveness.

I purposed to expand the definition beyond the ability to produce children. I wanted to be productive in every area, health, relationships, finances. The goal is total life prosperity, and I wanted it. I wanted to live. When you're gasping for breath, it's about survival. At the heart of the battle is the fight for your soul. So for a time I didn't focus on scriptures about barrenness. I made a shift and held tight to his word on prosperity in every area. I focused on His teachings on life. I had to choose.

Here are the scriptures I stood on to reclaim my life. None of them refer to giving birth. When you're fighting for your life, it's about self-preservation. You've got to save yourself.

The Word...

"Soon—and it will not be very long— the forests of Lebanon will become a fertile field, and the fertile field will yield bountiful crops." **(Isaiah 29:17 NLT)**

48

"Beloved, I pray that you may prosper in all things and be in health, just as your soul prospers." **(III John 1:2 NKJV)**

"See, I set before you today life and prosperity, death and destruction. For I command you today to love the Lord your God, to walk in obedience to him, and to keep his commands, decrees and laws; then you will live and increase, and the Lord your God will bless you in the land you are entering to possess." **(Deuteronomy 30:15-16 NIV)**

The scriptures above are a sampling of the powerful truth that ministered to me. The Lord used His word to teach; anytime I looked He was there. Through Bible study, films, friends, books, He always had something to say. Even His silence contained subtle clues to discover.

The breakdown...

The field of your life will produce. The seeds you sow will flower. It won't be long. Your health is important. It's part of your spiritual inheritance. Your physical and spiritual growth are connected. It's easy to favor one at the cost of the other. Strive for prosperity in every area. Keeping a holistic view will give balance. Choose life. Be intentional about how you want to live, especially when facing trials. You get to choose. Choose God.

The Prayer...

Lord, you've given me a choice. I choose life. I vow fertility in every area. I am prosperous in every area. I powerfully choose, with purpose and intention – to live. Amen.

For Reflection...

As you believe for God's best, what scriptures have you held close? What truths resonate with you?

Can you forgive betrayal? Can you make peace with your body during infertility?

Your body is your friend. You'll spend a lifetime in it. You rely on it without thinking. You ask it to run 5k's with no preparation, it responds automatically to most requests and goes beyond anything you could imagine to protect itself. Your body is your friend. Its systematic functioning is called upon to rule your physical experience of life on earth, but you only get one. You'll have to forgive her. She may not meet your expectations.

The relationship between a woman and her body is complex and ever-changing. From the budding of breasts and curves to the all-important question of when "it" will arrive, you've patterned a way of communicating with your body. You feel you know her - until you don't. Can you forgive her betrayal if she refuses to produce children - the perceived culmination of your womanly journey?

Infertility brings into question the authenticity of your relationship with your body. How well do you really know her? In crisis, can she be relied upon? The loss of a baby through miscarriage, inconsistent ovulation, tumors, and cysts - a million little things and a million little ways our bodies can fail us. And it only takes one. One experience of failure can make us question whether God's word is true. Betrayal can do that. The fearfully and wonderfully made body as described in the Bible? Clearly you didn't get one of those.

Infertility is the cruelest form of betrayal to the woman who desires a child. Your body can feel like a friend who betrayed you. A few months ago, and inspired by **Idelette McVicker** of **She Loves Magazine,** I wrote a love letter to my body. I wish I'd done this sooner. Something about rewinding the clock to review our relationship helped me process my feelings and examine the complexities of our connection. Until then, I felt only a general haze of anger towards my body because of infertility and its imperfections as viewed by a ballerina. Writing my feelings down was the beginning of a long overdue conversation with and about my body. Owning my feelings by writing them down changed me. I inched toward forgiveness and solidified my peace with God.

The Word...

"But you see in the dark because daylight and dark are all the same to you. You are the one who put me together inside my mother's body, and I praise you because of the wonderful way you created me. Everything you do is marvelous! Of this I have no doubt." – **(Psalm 139:12-14)**

The Prayer...

Lord, I am fearfully and wonderfully made. Infertility makes me doubt this truth. Encourage the development of my value around a solid hope in you - as center of all. Disentangle my thoughts from those of the world where beauty and worth are tied only to the physical. I want to be more like you. I want to be beautiful because of you. Link your spirit to mine. Ever intertwined. Lord I am yours, fearfully and wonderfully made - always. Dear beautiful body, I forgive you. I love you. Amen.

For reflection:

Write a love letter to your body. It doesn't have to be elaborate and you don't have to call yourself a writer. Just

write. Communicate gratitude for your body. I promise you'll be glad you did.

Here's mine...

Mesmerized by beauty and strength and finding a particularly sweet loveliness in small but significant treasures, I called myself a lover of women. A hand gesture, a pair of shoulders, the wonder of a beautifully captivating smile – I love women. But as my own worst critic, I found little time to revel in the unique set of mystery and power that was labeled Lisha and gifted to me by the God of creation.

Dear Body,

I'm not sure I loved you, not if what I feel for you now... can be compared to what I felt for you then.

I was a professionally trained dancer and compared my limbs, feet, hips...arms to those of world-class ballerinas, asking you to emulate their lines, their form, their style. I asked you dance to a different beat, a forced rhythm, you were unable to catch your breath.

Countless hours spent in open-air dance studios sweating, glistening, pushing. I must have been quite pretty because hard work is beautiful, and I've never worked so hard in my life. Everything right was always over-shadowed by the revelation that some things were wrong. I wish I could hug that tender, fragile version of myself - the dancer that desired only to be good enough. I was too busy asking you to be someone else. I was never satisfied with you. I became my mirrored reflection, always pushing, always asking for more. I wanted more. Higher, longer, stronger, faster. Never enough, just more.

I got caught in this ugly comparison cycle, a nasty game of constantly changing rules where no matter what happens or what I do, I lose. I lose myself when I lose you, and this has gone on for most of my adult life. I played and I lost.

After years of comparison, correction, and contorting, after molding and beating you into shape, I asked you to bring forth children.

You denied my request. I don't blame you, but for a while, I was angry and disappointed: the ugly disappointment that breeds jealousy and envy. Bitter feelings force love into a box never to be opened. Jealousy and envy are afraid. And fear cannot love.

I had major surgery twice. My uterus was ripped apart and put back together again to remove growths that may have multiplied as the years of self-loathing increased. After this, I asked you to give me children. And you refused. For fourteen years.

Maybe that's how long it took to fully heal from the trauma you experienced. Not even my prayers elicited the healing I sought. You needed time. I can hear you say so clearly: "I need time". You needed restoration, redemption, and anointing but all would flow according to His time.

In the meantime, my heart bore three souls. These are my spirit babies, my soul's longing for children made manifest in the lives of babes housed and born of other wombs - by women with other stories. My longing was so intense that the meditations of my heart coursed through their veins. Yes, if not my DNA, then certainly my prayers. I've always loved my heart, the part of me, that's most like Him. Not because I try, my efforts amount to very little, but because this heart has been washed and knows intimately of His love.

When you finally agreed to the promise of life, to carry it to fulfillment and see it through fruition - I barely believed in you.

We were not on speaking terms. I doubted you. I had little faith in you.

But...

I believed in Him.

The baby born of this promise is almost three. All boy. All life. All love. I bear scars from another battle now. This time my uterus was split open wide allowing my gift to spring forth - all love - all life -all boy. My warrior wound reminds me of my love for you. No longer unrequited, unreciprocated, a one way and very lonely highway. You love me and of this I am sure. You renewed my faith, not only because of the blessing of a son but because of the powerful lesson learned. You taught me that when given time and a little room for maturation, the subsequent healing belongs, not to the physical alone, but to the spirit as well. All things, all things - heal.

Dear body of mine...

You are loved.

Are you on speaking terms with your body? What can you do now to show your body love? Have you experienced a profound healing of body, mind, or spirit?

Do You Have a Plan?

When you're on the battle-field of infertility, the goal is to slay the dragon. Other warriors have gone before you with definitive plans for success. Some return triumphant; others were defeated; still others revise the plan mid-battle, calling a truce. What will you do? Do you have a plan? How will you slay the dragon?

We enter every war with a different game plan, and each warrior must define first, for herself, what winning means. Hopeful news arrives from the frontlines. If you go into the battle with a plan for parenthood, the odds are in your favor for success. With God on your side, you have every reason to plan for victory. Seek his will and make a plan.

There have been many advances in medical treatment for infertility. The majority of couples (65 percent) who enter the battlefield with a plan for treatment will be successful in giving birth. But only 44 percent of infertile couples seek treatment. If these numbers say anything, it's worth giving it a try. If God gives you peace about seeking medical assistance for the disease of infertility, go for it. The odds are on your side. God won't be mad at you, and your faith in him isn't on the line. He uses medical professionals to treat diseases. Infertility is one of them.

If science isn't your cup of tea, perhaps you'll consider adoption. Everything you wanted to know about it can be found on the family building resource section at **Resolve** or connect with me for more information. I am the mama of three through domestic adoption and will joyfully share my testimony and any information you might find useful. A reminder ... don't sit on this option. Some consider it the final frontier, something they can always do in the future. They sit on this idea until the very last minute, and sometimes that's a mistake. There are age limitations in adoption. Each agency has their own cut offs, but they do exist. Use this "ace-in-the-hole" wisely.

You may want to test the waters with foster care or feel God's tug on your heart for ministry in this area. Most foster care agencies operate now with permanence in mind. Realizing a forever family is best for a child; social workers go to great lengths to keep birth families together but are mindful of this fact. As a potential parent, you aren't necessarily last on the list. The system has its flaws, but if you're led in this calling - you've been anointed for the work. Believe God's best for the children you have the opportunity to love on, even if only for a season.

Child-free living is an option and is a powerful choice for those who feel called of God in this direction. This, to me, is the boldest choice and I respect the women who have bravely made the decision to experience a full life as a woman without children. The women I know who have made this choice have the freedom to reinvent themselves again and again. Their lives are full and rich with purpose.

Here's another scenario: you try all the treatments, potential adoptions fall through, and your heart still burns for the love of a child. You think the plan failed. What then? Believe God. He is the final authority over the plan of your life. There is hope and His plan never fails. Expand your vision to see beyond natural circumstances. He is always at work in your life. Find ways to satisfy your longing by investing in the lives of the little people around you. Or dismiss the idea of having children and embrace freedom from the responsibility of raising them. Enjoy the valuable position held by women without children. Try not to worry. Change is inevitable. Stay in faith. Stay focused.

Whatever you decide, do your research. In His word and online. Revelation and information is readily available, and none of us living in this unique time in history should be able to say, "I didn't know "about anything. He promises to give wisdom, and He gives it freely.

The Word...

"For I know the plans that I have for you,' declares the Lord, 'plans for welfare and not for calamity to give you a future and a hope." **(Jeremiah 29:11)**

"God did this according to his eternal plan. And he was able to do what he had planned because of all that Christ Jesus our Lord had done." **(Ephesians 3:11)**

These songs...

I've got my feet shod, With the preparation of peace
Got my sword of the Spirit, My shield of faith
Got my breastplate of righteousness, Helmet of salvation
I put on my armor, And I'm ready for the battle

Order my steps in Your Word, Dear Lord
Lead me, guide me every day
Send Your anointing, Father, I pray
Order my steps in Your Word, yes
Order my steps in Your Word

The Prayer...

Lord, I'm on the battlefield, and I need a plan. I want to know your will. Order my steps, each according to your divine plan. I ask for revelation, favor, and direction. I'll move when you say move. I'll sit still when you ask. I'm resting in the depths of

your love. Align my will with yours. I don't fear the future.
Your plan is my prosperity. Amen.

For Reflection…

Write out your plan. Read books and blogs about women in similar circumstances. Be inspired by their journeys and ask God to direct yours. Make a plan. Write it out. Call your doctor … again.

What songs inspire you? What songs get you through?

Walking by Faith

If you generally don't speak to anyone about infertility, just picking up this book and making it to this point is huge. You're having the internal dialogue. You're dealing with it. But you may still be in the trenches. Struggling with believing God when circumstances refute everything he says. This chapter is for you.

On the battlefield, you have to fight for your faith.

The plan of action isn't only a practical plan of steps to motherhood. The plan of action is to stay alive, with your faith intact.

When the battle rages, how do you hold onto your faith? When you don't get pregnant, when you miscarry, when your husband doesn't want to pursue adoption or a potential match falls through, when the third round of IVF doesn't work, or when your prayers feel unheard and seemingly go unanswered? When your dreams of motherhood have not survived beyond the realm of your imagination ... what then? What of your faith?

Faith is built in the day-by-day little things, the overlooked, the mundane. Begin to thank Him for the little things. If you can shift your focus from "please give me" to "thank you for," you've made a successful transition to a life of gratitude.

Faith grows. God will show up. His presence and activity in your life is a sure thing, but you'll have to trust. Problems arise when we don't see him moving quickly enough and in the way we thought he would. A large part of the development of faith is learning to wait. Start with the little things and build toward a life of gratitude and patience. If we could see everything, see into the future to know exactly how things would turn out, there'd be no reason for faith.

You can't explain your faith. It's part of your inner knowing, your connection with spirit. With God. Your mind can't rationalize it, thereby proving it. The commentary passage below nails it.

"Faith proves to the mind, the reality of things that cannot be seen by the bodily eye. It is a full approval of all God has revealed, as holy, just, and good." - **Matthew Henry's Concise Commentary**

The Word...

"The fundamental fact of existence is that this trust in God, this faith, is the firm foundation under everything that makes life worth living. It's our handle on what we can't see. The act of faith is what distinguished our ancestors, set them above the crowd. By faith, we see the world called into existence by God's word, what we see created by what we don't see." **(Hebrews 11:1-3, MSG)**

Let's dig a little deeper...

Our spiritual eyes give us vision and hope for the future. We have to use them. But we have a choice: to pursue fulfillment of His promise or turn away, broken by the nagging ache of dreams left to die. This shift in focus is important because we have to want our relationship with him more than anything. More than anything. More than the baby. (I know that hurts and I'm sorry. But it's true *hugs*)

Dig deep. Fight like your life depends on it because it does. Work your faith, believe God.

Faith is knowing and believing. Not wavering and doubting.

What you believe determines your actions. Without faith, you won't move. Without faith, you won't seek treatment, you won't attend an information session at an adoption agency. Without faith, you'll never try. And what of the women who never try? They wind up bitter and deeply bruised because an important part of them has died. Your faith is your breath. Faith is the reason we live and proclaim His love. Hold onto your faith.

The Prayer…

Lord, I'm at a crossroads. My faith is weak, and I spend more and more time wondering. I want to believe you. I know how important it is to believe, but reality gets in the way. I doubt. I do. A part of me knows your goodness, knows you're real. My mind can't rationalize that feeling away. So I wait for you. I work my faith and wait. Amen.

A Story…

It was Christmas, and the long drive out to southern New Jersey made my legs cramp and tingle. I jumped out of my seat, folding arms around my most valued possession. That year, I was happy. That year, I had a baby to hold. I made a beeline for the entrance. Making my way to my brother's always open door, I trudged through fresh fallen snow.

Cold rushed in behind me but couldn't compete with their cozy home. I pushed the door shut with my free arm and enjoyed the heart -warming feeling of family, of home. Surrounded by faces I love, I looked up to see my sister-in-law coming down the stairs. She had just given birth to their third child … a boy. And I had forgotten the particular sting a new baby brings to a woman who cannot birth her own children. I was in love with my son and fulfilled, in so many ways when I remembered: adoption isn't a cure for infertility. It healed my hurt but didn't cure the longing.

Over her shoulder she held him, swaddled in a thin tan blanket. I could smell him. Before she reached me, I imagined the softness of his skin, the tender curl of his hair. I wasn't done. The longing was intense and moved me to hopeful, happy tears. I lowered my eyes to hide tears I could never explain. That night I knew there'd be another baby in my world. And so began another season of waiting.

This season of waiting would be different though. I'd learned how to do it.

Winter is for waiting.

It's cold as I write, and NYC is covered in a blanket of snow. Outside, several inches cling to branches over-laden with leaves. They bend, giving in to the weight of their unexpected burden.

But it's beautiful and important. The shimmering softness and powdery glitter hint at stories in this airy wonderland. It feels magical and weightless. But tiny leaves and thin branches have another story to tell. They're holding on.

Look closely. Each snowflake is unique though veiled in a blanket of uniformity. And today's snow-fall won't look the same tomorrow. In fact, each storm is new and will never come again. Winter is a perpetual pause, a forced interruption before the wild rush of spring. Winter wills us to wait in expectancy. A tender shoot. A fragile twig. The elusive bud. Winter demands … spring.

It's broken, brittle, and cracked. Lulled by this cyclical suspension, winter forces us inside. We crave shelter, a covering and protection from danger. We retreat to prepare for the hopeful promise of spring. But first we wait.

Winter is a season of waiting. Powdery hills and drifts camouflage life. And bare trees crush optimism. Winter covers or strips; either way, our view is obstructed … we find it hard to see.

Winter is hard not hopeless.

Winter tests our faith and the promise of spring comes with this truth: Not every tree will bloom. Not every bud will blossom. But we're born to believe, and winter makes us wrestle. We long for a faith that's whole. Desperate to believe, we settle in to let God do the work, mending the cracks in our fragmented faith. In winter, we swallow the word whole and simply, beautifully, TRUST.

That winter was different, that winter I embraced the quiet. I didn't worry about the wait.

The stillness and silence of a world gone cold is perfect for restoration. Before the breakthrough, we'd do well to replenish. It's the ideal time to renew our faith, to prepare our hearts to again … BELIEVE.

Winter is for wisdom. Let's use it wisely.

No questions today. Sending hugs and love.

The Infertile Stepmother

When Rodney and I married, I became the step-mother of his then fourteen-year-old son. Rodney's mother was no longer living, and his father was never a part of his life. His family, the new family I would forever be connected to, was his son and his son's mother. Nothing traditional about this. But it was also completely ordinary. We were just one example of the new modern family.

Life was good until we began a years long journey to conceive. I became an infertile stepmother. Nothing could prepare me for the frustration I would feel being an infertile "second wife." I didn't think it could get any worse. Until my step-son had a son.

Thank God the kitchen counter was there to steady me. Phone to ear, I tensed. My shoulders crouched towards my ears, and I felt every muscle in my body respond to the words. Emoni, my step-son was a father. His son was born a few weeks after my thirty-seventh birthday.

I was an infertile stepmother and now grandmother to my stepson's child. I wasn't ready. This was an unwanted and very painful layer of head-tripping for a woman going through infertility. Emoni, to me, was physical evidence that the fertility problems we had were mine. He, like his dad, was long, tall, and lanky. He would walk into a room and all I imagined was everyone looking, not at him, but at me. Wasn't I supposed to give him a sibling, his father a child? Every year I failed, my barrenness became more of an ugly addition to the stereotypical image of the evil stepmother.

We were in a happy place when Emoni's son was born. LiChai, our first child through adoption, had arrived two years earlier, and I was living my dream as a mama. But that news still shocked me and brought with it a new level of pain. My infertility hurt in a way it hadn't before. My stepson was privileged to bring life into the world, and all I felt was the weight of the injustice. What could be fair about this?

I don't know how I attended the baby welcoming ceremony or how I embraced his child as a grandmother. To be honest, I don't think I fully have. I was uncomfortable and broken in a way that made me feel useless. All I could think about was myself, which clouded the joy I might have experienced if joy could be found in such a place. But I might have had peace. Peace would have been good.

So I did what everyone does. Hurt people, hurt people. So my sweet Christian girl soul sat back in judgment. I judged everything about his situation and found the sweet spot of the lofty when I decided to feel *sorry* for him.

But really I was jealous, and those feelings stayed with me a long time. This chapter is hard to write because I'm still working through this. Nine years later I still have strong feelings about how I'd like things to change.

I want to be a grandmother to his children (you heard it right, Emoni also has a daughter now). The dynamics of his situation, combined with my real world experience of full-time parenting, makes that hard.

I've pushed past my judgmental stance and now pray to be part of their lives.

I could look back in regret, and there is a bit of that, but I have to move forward. In today's modern family, I have to embrace the life I have and the children God's blessed me with. All of them. I have to walk in love. Period.

The Word...

"Elkanah had two wives, Hannah and Peninnah. Although Peninnah had children, Hannah did not have any." **(1 Samuel 1:2)**

"He causes the barren woman of the house to dwell as the happy mother of children. Praise the Lord!" **(Psalms 113:9 NKJV)**

The Prayer...

Lord, I'm walking a hard road. I don't know how to mother my husband's children. They remind me of my barrenness, and I'm jealous of a gift you've already granted him. One you've denied me. Not being able to share in the joy of pregnancy and birth with my husband makes infertility even harder. In a way, it divides us. I still don't understand, and I'm hurt. I need your help. Bring something beautiful out of this mess. Heal the hurt, mend the broken. Your word says you will. Amen.

If you're an infertile stepmother...

I hope sharing my story encourages you to make choices you can be happy with. Walk in love and pray continually for peace. With that, I think you'll do fine. I'm praying for you.

Day Off: Love

*"Love makes your soul crawl out from its hiding place." - **Zora Neale Hurston***

Today I want to talk about love.

I listened to the ministry teaching of **Michael T. Smith** recently. Funny and engaging, he talked about love and the gospel. He also talked about how we don't get to define love. We don't get to pick and choose what we feel about love. Combining those elements, the gospel of truth plus our own ideas about love – will never equal love, no matter how much we believe them. Because we don't get to define love. God does.

I'm thinking about love. What and who I love, how I express it. I'm wondering if my version of love lines up with the gospel of truth. Because I think the preacher was right - we don't get to define love. God is love. And his love always lines up with his word. His love is beautifully made.

The last chapter was hard. I shared a challenging part of my love walk, an area where I'm asked to go beyond the superficial to the painful and ugly parts of relationships. To the explosive space between my head and heart where the ugliness of emotion rules. Love doesn't, love won't - live there. I want to love like Jesus, but what does that look like?

How do we allow Him to manifest his love through us - to others? Because that's what we're called to do: to respond in love to life. Every day and in a million ways, we practice love through life. Every experience and trial is a call to respond in love. Every answer of love is a cry of yes to the One who *is* love. He is the definition of love.

Is God using you as His hands and heart? To bless and encourage or remain in relationship with others, especially when it's hard? How is He refining your definition of love? Does it look more like His? On your day off, will you challenge yourself (in the giving and receiving) to love better? The benefit is a more beautiful you.

The Word...

"Love never gives up. Love cares more for others than for self. Love doesn't want what it doesn't have. Love doesn't strut, Doesn't have a swelled head, Doesn't force itself on others, Isn't always "me first," Doesn't fly off the handle, Doesn't keep score of the sins of others, Doesn't revel when others grovel, Takes pleasure in the flowering of truth, Puts up with anything, Trusts God always, Always looks for the best, Never looks back, But keeps going to the end. Love never dies. Inspired speech will be over some day; praying in tongues will end; understanding will reach its limit." **(1 Corinthians 13:4-8)**

The Prayer...

Lord, you are the definition of love. As your hands and heart in the earth, I want to be love. Make real this sweet gift – a tangible expression of you. Persistent. Raw. Relentless. Redemptive. Encourage me in the pursuit of your word. It's there; I'll find it. I want to love without fear, loosen my grasp, open my hand to receive your outpouring of love. Amen.

For Reflection…

What comes to mind when you hear the word love? Is there anyone in your life you can love better?

Miscarriage

Miscarriage is unexplainable and to the woman going through it, the deepest of losses. It's not easy to explain or express how in love you were. Even if only for a few days or weeks.

A friend miscarried recently, and I felt the heart-break of her loss. Baby - no baby. Life pulsating and pushing forth, embedded in your core and then - not. Like I said, it's the most difficult feeling to explain. Think of the sudden popping of every balloon or float at a parade. There was every reason for a party and then...there wasn't. What happened? Somewhere a soul had taken residence within, and now that soul has left. It really is the most deflating, defeating, depression inducing event a woman can experience.

My heart broke for her because I know how all this feels, and I hate knowing anyone has to go through it.

I want to tell her the truth. If you hold onto God, all will be well. That, I can promise. This is rock-solid truth embedded in what's left of a refurbished heart. I know this and share it. But I also know that part of this truth is a pain I can't minimize. I won't minimize her loss by fumbling for words. "These things happen" and "it was God's plan "empty, rote, form letter fill-ins. Sometimes there are no words. I'll pray quietly and offer the only thing I can think of. I'll help hold her heart with a hug-filled "I'm sorry." Because I think it best she have her cry. A good cry is the beginning of healing.

The first time it happened to me I put on a brave face, pretending all was well. These things happen; you know the drill. I kept silent, bought into the "women's work" motto, and hitched up my big girl panties. Back to work and the grind of life.

But it wasn't okay, and it wouldn't be for years. The dark place where I took residence held no life, no light, and no room for dreams. It was clear I'd fallen out favor. God couldn't love people who live there. How could he? This was my fault. Doubt and fear were constant companions. I lived here. Alone. I didn't feel love. I didn't feel loved.

And that's exactly the way our enemy would like it.

With miscarriage, silence is deadly. Though it's expected, the hushed tones and dismissal of a topic categorized as unspeakable, make a hard thing – even harder. We don't talk about it. It's sad and makes us uncomfortable. The death of a baby is like that. My fingers shook on the keys, and I held my breath just typing the words "death ... baby." No one wants to hear what or how it happened. It's too much information. Private and personal. But no less traumatizing than the loss of a hand. More so.

But we should talk about it. Because the life was real, and attached to the other end of the severed cord is a woman ... broken. She needs to tell her story. She should be heard. Her story is redemptive and tied forever in truth. Her story can heal.

But you can't heal what you don't acknowledge as hurt.

Without acknowledgement of pain we can't tell the story. The story so many of us hide. It's only in personal initiation in the club that you hear the quiet echoes of "you too?" Then we remember due dates, and names and if you really want to know we'll tell you about the children we hold in heaven and our last day together.

We have to tell the stories.

We are the ones who know intimately the faith needed for every day. We understand the gift and hope of each week of pregnancy. We're the ones who know time stopping silence. We wait in holy anticipation for the steadfast synchronicity of a heartbeat. We are the ones who watch our doctors for any nuance or change in tone. We know the looks when all is well, and we know the look that says it's not.

Every birth is a miracle, and women who experience loss acknowledge the sacred, holy wonder of creation differently. Our perspective is forever changed, and we should share it. Because of it, we grow into grateful mothers. We become prayer warriors for other women and the children we hope for. We learn compassion. We gain strength. The world wouldn't know how precious; how miraculous the life process is if they didn't hear stories like ours. Who better to hear those stories from than us?

I'm proud of my friend. She isn't going through this alone. She has a virtual team of sisters praying for her restoration. She's going through her process, and I know all will be well. Miscarriage is an opportunity for a sovereign God to minister grace to his daughters. And really, only He can do that.

In the meantime, I'll speak truth and pray.
All will be well.
In the telling is the liberating power of redemption.
In the telling is ... hope.

The Word...

"He heals the broken-hearted and binds up their wounds. He determines the number of the stars and calls them each by name. Great is our Lord and mighty in power; His understanding has no limit." **(Psalm 147:3-5)**

"He (God) Himself has said, I will not in any way fail you nor give you up nor leave you without support. I will not, I will not, I will not, in any degree leave you helpless, nor forsake nor let you down, relax my hold on you – assuredly not!" **(Hebrews 13:5)**

The Prayer...

The loss of my unborn child leaves me speechless. There. Are. No. Words. Only my heart's cry. Wrap me in your arms. Amen.

Take me to that place Lord

To that secret place where

I can be with You

You make me like You

*Wrap me in Your arms, wrap me in Your arms, Wrap me in Your arms – **Freddy Rodriquez***

To build your faith up to believe for a child again here are a few resources

- Hannah's Prayer Ministries
- New Life Ministries

Watch Your Words

"I can't carry a child."

"Obviously I'm no fertile Myrtle."

"I guess it isn't in His plan."

"I don't even want to get pregnant now. I'm too old anyway."

My head was filled with thoughts like these. And I thought they were based on facts because I'd experienced miscarriage, believed my present reality was a foretelling of the future, and was over 35. With words, I wrote the ending of my fertility journey without asking God.

I'd talked to him about it. But when I didn't get the answer I wanted, I picked up the pen and started writing for myself. I tried out my thoughts – speaking without thinking. Not realizing the power of my words I'd say whatever I felt. I was "keeping it real" *just* "being honest" but I was digging my own grave.

We have to watch our words. Our words create our reality. They are the manifestation of our thoughts and the bounty of our hearts. Everything we do and are is because of our words.

I learned this life-changing lesson and changed the course of my destiny.

It takes time. You have to retrain your brain. Renew your mind. I renewed my mind with God's word. I replaced my negative thoughts with His word. Starting with little things like a shift in perspective, I chose to render any situation a possibility. I stopped being so pessimistic about my desire to conceive. I began with a shrug of the shoulders and said things like "you never know." In response to positive comments from others, I'd offer "from your mouth to Gods ears." I know it doesn't sound like much, but moving from such a negative space is hard. I was slowly bringing my thoughts into captivity.

From there I'd make declarations and memorize scripture pertaining to my situation. I was learning to love myself again. My love tank was being refilled. My heart restored. It took a long time, but a tiny seed of hope sprung forth with new life. And with hope anything is possible. My vision for the future was bright. I hoped it would include giving birth to a biological child but I was no longer consumed with the idea. I was confident in the joy I was experiencing. I was at peace.

Has your season of waiting turned your thought process into a constant stream of mental parrying, a negative wave of emotions you feel free to give voice to? There's nothing wrong with sharing your feelings. We should all have a safe place to share our troubles. Godly relationships provide that encouragement. However, if those fear based thoughts have become your life's mantra, you've crossed a line. Wrong thinking can ruin your life. It's simple. Change your thinking. Change your life.

The Word...

"Casting down imaginations, and every high thing that exalteth itself against the knowledge of God, and bringing into captivity every thought to the obedience of Christ;" **(2 Corinthians 10:5 (KJV)**

"Do not conform to the pattern of this world, but be transformed by the renewing of your mind. Then you will be able to test and approve what God's will is—his good, pleasing and perfect will." (**Romans 12:2**)

"The tongue has the power of life and death, and those who love it will eat its fruit." (**Proverbs 18:21 (NIV)**)

The Prayer...

Lord, I'm filled with negative thoughts. I have to watch my words. I struggle with expressing myself and speaking your truth. My head and heart are at odds. And I know it's wrong. Engaging in a cycle of doubt and fear by saying everything I "feel" won't make things better. Renew my mind. Let my thoughts be yours. I need a fresh revelation of hope. Lord set my heart to hope in You. Amen.

For Reflection...

How have negative thoughts kept you from moving forward?

Stay in the word. Create a positive mantra to replace the negative stream. It can be as simple as "No" in response to destructive thoughts. The point is to train your heart and mind to believe Gods' word.

For The Day You Curse God

Because of wrong thinking, you'll spend a lot of time trapped in fear and doubt. This can happen, even while working hard to renew your mind. A negative medical report, yet another pregnancy announcement: any of these things can push you to the edge. Pent up anger only builds, and one day you'll be at your lowest level of faith. You'll hit rock bottom. You'll know you're there because that is the day you'll curse God.

Maybe you'll find out your fifteen-year-old niece is expecting. Perhaps the doctor will tell you the fibroids you had surgery to remove twice have grown back. Maybe you'll be diagnosed with a rare clotting disorder, making pregnancy unlikely. I don't know what your mountain will be, what crevice you'll encounter as you are forced to climb. But you will face one.

I have to be completely honest with you. The day you face the mountain will be hard. And you will want to give up. Full of bitterness, you'll turn your face from God and whisper the deepest level of doubt. "I don't believe you."

He promises to hold you anyway. Grace will rush in and fill the chasm, seal the gap, satiate the gorge. The crack runs deep, but God is greater. He'll bring you over and through.

Take the test. The testing of your faith leads to a beautiful river of hope. Each faith test yields that much more. And all you need is a mustard seed.

The other side of the mountain? I don't know. But He does. The promise is that whatever it is you face; all will be well. On the other side is peace.

This isn't to say we should feel free to curse God. To be clear, what I am saying is this: grace is available. When you begin to comprehend the depth of His love for you, you won't want to curse Him. He'll turn your curse to praise. Let Him.

I want to encourage you to hold on. No matter how hard it gets or how much anger you feel, just hold on. God is bigger than the day you give up.

The Word...

"I'll never let you down, never walk off and leave you." **(Hebrews 13:5)**

"By entering through faith into what God has always wanted to do for us—set us right with him, make us fit for him—we have it all together with God because of our Master Jesus. And that's not all: We throw open our doors to God and discover at the same moment that he has already thrown open his door to us. We find ourselves standing where we always hoped we might stand—out in the wide open spaces of God's grace and glory, standing tall and shouting our praise." **(Romans 5:1-2), MSG** * *Read all the way through verse 11 if you can. It's really good! *

"And I am sure of this, that he who began a good work in you will bring it to completion at the day of Jesus Christ." **(Philippians 1:6)**

The Prayer...

Lord, forgive me. In my anger, I've cursed you. My soul's cry is for your sovereign plan. Not my will - yours. I want your blessing. I need your grace. Forgiveness is free, and I receive it. Turn my curse to praise. You are. And I am yours. Eternally. Amen.

The Shift

When you make it past the day you curse God, and you will, a shift will take place. Your focus will shift from you to God and his word. You'll spend more time being hopeful, more time feeling confident in your portion and excited about the wondrous possibility of the future. The question mark that hung over your head is no longer filled with fear. It's a symbol of hope.

This shift is an act of grace. The seismic transformation signals the beginning of a new day.

I made the shift when I opened my heart to other options for family building. My husband and I had discussed adoption while dating. But baby lust is strong, and for a time, I couldn't see my way around the beauty of a pregnant belly. Finally, I opened my heart, letting loose much of the tension I carried, and focused on what he was telling me to do. From that point on, I knew I'd be a mama ... someday. My chances for success expanded exponentially when I made the shift.

Lust is a good word for the desperate desire we feel when walking through infertility. Our hearts ache in an ugly way for something we don't have. That crippling ache is not from God. The baby becomes an idol. Above and before Him. The shift can't take place with a baby or anything else in that gap. The gap can only be filled by Him.

Adoption is pretty dramatic. My shift happened with a bold leap that included the lives of people I'd never met. But opening your heart to adoption isn't the only way to make the shift.

We tend to look for sensational, exaggerated shifts in the universe, we expect wind and torrential rain all around. But sometimes the storm is quiet, an inner spiritual storm of gentle rains and whispered winds. However you experience the storm, it can be settled with His word. The shift happens with the acceptance of truth. It's possible to wake up and just "get it." The transformation in us is huge, but how it happens may be subtle, peaceful and quiet, but no less impactful. God loves us each uniquely. He creatively connects with our hearts, speaks a language we each can hear. Listen for it.

Have you made the shift? God can't work until you do.

The Word...

"Here's what I want you to do: find a quiet, secluded place so you won't be tempted to role play before God. Just be there as simply and honestly as you can manage. The focus will shift from you to God, and you will begin to sense his grace." (**Matthew 6:6, MSG**)

The Prayer...

Lord, thank you for change. It was a hard road, but I made the shift. You were there with grace to make it happen. But I had to choose. Now, I look to you. Keep me. It's easy to fall back into old patterns of thinking, to forget your transformative work. Help me remember your love, to walk in your grace. Amen.

How Will Motherhood Find You?

Sometimes motherhood is planned - each detail written and played in time and tune like the notes of a magnificent symphony. Other times it comes by surprise - a door suddenly opening, forcing you to jump uncontrollably, in a rush to answer. Motherhood can come unexpectedly, and in ways we might never imagine.

Most often, the call to motherhood is whispered in the secret place, where our outward displays of success and accomplishment mean nothing. It's here we find ourselves bare. We are confronted with a primal desire to nurture and care for, to give selflessly, to love on a level never known. No matter how you experience it, the call is undeniable. You want to be a mother.

For many, "I want to" becomes "I will be." An undeniable passion. A God-sized dream you just can't let go of.

Each woman walks her own path, yet, arrival at this point is crucial because the woman who prayerfully identifies her desire will fight for motherhood with renewed purpose. Fighting a battle when victory is assured gives confidence to keep pushing when obstacles come your way, or when you simply get tired. No longer stuck on an image of "the perfect" or "the traditional," you are free to explore your options. Motherhood will find you because you've opened your heart to receive and believe for an unplanned, unexplained miracle.

Thoughts on Surrender

If you're a dreamer like me, the word surrender is not at the top of your list of favorites. To surrender means to let go, give up, abandon hope. No way! Not for dreamers like us. Right?

Preparing to wade into the waters of adoption, I hesitated. Pause. What happens if I let go of the baby dream? Does it mean I'll never give birth? Never have a baby? How do I let go of this dream - a dream that almost feels like my baby? How do I give it all up - the late nights I gently rocked and nursed it, praying, planning and preparing for it, believing for my miracle?

After the devastating late loss of a cherished pregnancy, I found myself in the ring, wrestling with God. I resisted. I cried. But eventually, I got the message. I would have to surrender my dream to find His. His will. His plan. My destiny designed *by Him*, with no input from me. I would have to surrender.

I drank deeply of the meaning of this word when I met my son's birthmother. I don't compare my loss with hers, but I do consider it and have been challenged by it. People often talk heroically about the hands that stand readily to give, but ponder for a moment the hands surrendered to receive. Suffice it to say, the heart must be in a special place to survive such a wave of grace. We met in a place of unspeakable pain, two women with separate sorrows. But oh the surrender ... we met at the point of surrender. That day, we each let go of something. She, the sweet child she birthed, and I, myself as the bearer of my would-be baby. It was a life-transforming exchange, one that you don't get to prepare for. It leaves a mark that can never be erased. I let go of my fantasy mama to be a real one to the baby in my arms. God's plan was that I be his mother.

We had to let go to grab hold of the new dream God had planned for us. He blessed my willingness to follow Him. I should have released my plans long ago. They were black and white dreams, dull and void of depth. They were discarded, blank and crumpled canvases compared to the brilliant masterpiece He'd designed specifically for me. I am fortunate to have a connection with my son's birthmother and have peace knowing her painting glows just as brightly. Hers has different shades, tones, and textures, but it's just as colorful yes, colorful indeed. Her life is full and, in her words, rebuilt. New! We share a story of redemption through surrender.

The Word...

As you consider adoption, this is my prayer for you (because it's always about love)

"My response is to get down on my knees before the Father, this magnificent Father who parcels out all heaven and earth. I ask him to strengthen you by his Spirit—not a brute strength but a glorious inner strength—that Christ will live in you as you open the door and invite him in. And I ask him that with both feet planted firmly on love, you'll be able to take in with all followers of Jesus the extravagant dimensions of Christ's love. Reach out and experience the breadth! Test its length! Plumb the depths! Rise to the heights! Live full lives, full in the fullness of God." **(Ephesians 3:14-19)**

The Prayer...

Lord, I'm ready for motherhood. Children are a blessing and, no matter how they arrive, bring joy. I feel led to prayerfully consider adoption. I'm responding to this call with a resounding yes. Continue to develop the qualities I'll need to raise godly children. My arms are open. I'll carefully consider the options you place before me and surrender my plans for your will. Grant me favor that I might be a blessing. Thank you for the gift, even the dream, of motherhood. Amen.

What to Expect When You're Expecting after Infertility

*"A miracle is when the whole is greater than the sum of its parts. A miracle is when one plus one equals a thousand." - **Frederick Buechner***

A few weeks shy of my forty-fourth birthday I learned I was pregnant ... again. This had happened before, and I brushed it off as another setup for failure. I'd had another miscarriage two years prior. My body's last grasps at fertility were a cruel joke. Two pregnancies in my forties? What was this all about? I didn't expect this.

When I made it past fourteen weeks (my longest pregnancy), I allowed myself to imagine the possibility of meeting my baby. I began to expect him. I read scriptures, sang to, and prayed for him. I wanted him. Hoped for him. Toyed with the belief that our spirits would tangibly collide in the human realm. I wanted to touch him. I knew the others; I just hadn't touched them.

After the last miscarriage, I was done. I was forty-two and happily the mother of three through adoption. I'd had enough of this pregnancy thing and didn't expect my reproductive history would change. I cut my hair. I started taking care of my body again. I was walking towards resolution when I encountered God in pregnancy.

A pregnant, formerly infertile girl gets to know her God well. What better way for our relationship to crystallize, for Him to show me how much more he wanted from me? He wanted to fill my half-full glass and he did it by bringing me low and on my knees as I walked with him through pregnancy. He took me to the secret place.

We made it through thirty-three weeks and four days of pregnancy. My water broke after five weeks of bed rest. I like to think my son wanted to meet me just as much as I wanted to meet him. He was tiny. He was here. After eleven days in the NICU, I brought him home.

Pregnancy was scary. A million "what ifs" and the knowledge that things don't always work out kept me on edge. I never relaxed. His movement was the gift of pregnancy. As long as he moved and every time he did, I rejoiced. I knew God in those moments. I remember the first flutters and the core shaking rumblings they developed into. He was real.

I pray God grants you the miracle of pregnancy. My advice? Grab a few scriptures to hold onto. You'll need them. I carried a pocket copy of Jackie Mize's Supernatural Pregnancy everywhere I went. I read and re-read it cover-to-cover, marinating in the life-giving words of Gods promises, words that helped me expect the unexpected, believe the unbelievable.

Pregnancy after infertility is a faith ride. It's another step on the journey calling you, drawing you closer to the one who loves you most.

While searching for a link to Jackie Mize's book, I learned of her untimely passing. She impacted my life and so many others. Her pregnancy and infertility ministry were powerful tools the Lord used to bring forth miracles. I'm praying for her family and friends.

The Word...

"And did you know that your cousin Elizabeth conceived a son, old as she is? Everyone called her barren, and here she is six months pregnant! Nothing, you see, is impossible with God." **(Luke 1:36-37)**

The Prayer...

Lord, I'm pregnant. I'm living my dream, but I'm afraid. Memories of loss hold joy captive, and I impatiently search for a smile. Any day now ... a smile. But God, you are bigger than my emotions. I'll take this walk with you. I'll rest in your promise. I'm brought low with humility, stunned by your grace. Lord, I'm pregnant. Selah.

Have You Chosen to Be Still? Have You Found Yourself Living Child-free?

I have tremendous admiration for women who powerfully choose this path because this was not an option for me. Rather than being a single facet of a multidimensional life, our culture still cultivates the belief that women are incomplete without the title of mother. I struggled with this and couldn't find my happy place. I fought to define myself as a woman without children.

I wonder about women who, because of illness are faced with infertility - and too, of women who choose to live child-free. Do they feel robbed of a critical life experience? Have time and circumstance conspired against their plans for motherhood? Do they ultimately sink into resolve over a situation they've lost control of? More importantly I try not to project my dreams on another woman. I remember – not every woman wants to have a baby.

Yet I believe all women mother, spiritually if not physically. Women nurture. Before walking into motherhood through marriage, adoption, and birth I mothered as an aunt and godmother. It was always natural for me to give voice to my inner mother. She spoke and I transformed. From girl to woman, I tended and took care of. Mothering was always in me.

So it's hard to write about living child-free, to properly represent the women who didn't choose but find themselves still childless. It's also difficult to express the hard truth behind the decision to live without children. I want to honor the women who walk in this space. Their bravery astounds me. But I wonder? What lies on the other side of this choice, this reality? As with any decision, is there a possibility of regret and what does that look like?

A few insights on living child-free ...

One of my very favorite women crafted this self-portrait, one of many stories of a child-free life.

"I love children, and most kids that I know love me. I love the way babies pull my hair and my earrings and pinch the mole on my face, how they laugh with their whole bodies. The way toddlers document their experiences with crayons and paper and try to do everything the adults around them do. They really do make my heart melt. On the other hand, I'm blessed because when I'm done playing with them I get to give them back to mommy and daddy and go home to a quiet house, go on vacation when I want, stay out late, whatever it may be. I answer only to myself.
But I have to admit, within the last few months I have felt like something is missing in my life. I try to look into the future and it seems very lonely, no husband or children... While I believe it's possible I might meet someone great and get married again, I don't see myself being able to give birth simply because of my age. That thought doesn't really upset me. What I do find disturbing is that due to the type of childhood that I had, I never saw myself as a mother." - **Dawn Hewitt age 46**

This from the blog of Elizabeth Gilbert

"I have come to believe there are three sorts of women, when it comes to questions of maternity. There are women who are born to be mothers, women who are born to be aunties, and women who should not be allowed within ten feet of a child. It's really important to know which category you belong to ... Now, listen — if you put a baby in front of me, rest assured: that baby is

89

going to get cuddled, spoiled and adored. But even as I'm loving on that beautiful infant, I know in my heart: This is not my destiny. It never was. And there is a curious rush of joy that I feel, knowing this to be true—for it is every bit as important in life to understand who you are NOT, as to understand who you ARE. Me, I'm just not a mom ... Having reached a contented and productive middle age,

I can say without a blink of hesitation that I wouldn't trade my choices for anything."

And this from a writer at Christianity Today ...

*While we do see children as a blessing, we see them as a blessing that God gives to some people, not all. Some people don't have kids because they never marry. Some have to face heartbreaking infertility and can't have children. And others might not have kids because God blessed them with passions and gifts that give them the same sense of fulfillment and joy that their friends get from their children. There is nothing wrong with finding your main purpose in being a parent and raising children. But there also is nothing wrong with finding your purpose in something else. – **Emily Timbol***

The Word...

"The righteous shall flourish like a palm tree, he shall grow like a cedar of Lebanon. Those who are planted in the house of the Lord shall flourish in the courts of our God. They shall still bear fruit in old age; They shall be fresh and flourishing to declare that the Lord is upright; He is my rock, and there is no unrighteousness in Him." **(Psalms 92: 12-15)**

The Prayer…

Lord, I'm still here. My prayers for a child have gone before you, and I haven't received the answer I hoped for. Now, it almost feels too late. Still I trust you. So I'm redefining my life. I ask you to partner with me to birth something beautiful. Something uniquely mine. A life. Lord, I give my life to you. Again. Amen.

For Reflection…

Have you considered the possibility that children may not be in your future? Make the decision to sit with that thought for a minute. Pray for revelation concerning the fruit, according to His word, you *will* bear.

When You Face the End of Your Fertility Journey

This is the chapter that cuts the deepest because the topic unearths me, places me front and center in the now of my fertility journey. I include it here because although you may be at the beginning of your story, it will change. And there's beauty there, even in the uncertainty of an ever-evolving story.

So here it is...

One successful pregnancy wasn't enough for me. The beauty of a full belly and the experience of nursing made me want it again. In fact, I secretly hoped to conceive again, almost immediately after giving birth. Six weeks was too long to wait. I listened to and wanted to believe all the stories about heightened fertility after pregnancy. I wanted to do it again.

But there was a glitch. I wasn't sure if I wanted another baby or just the experience of pregnancy. Actually having a living baby gave me confidence in my body's ability. This was refreshing after infertility, which had made me doubt my body in a way that made me feel ugly and unworthy. And there had been so many fears. I didn't walk through my pregnancy the way people do now. There were no posts on Facebook, no public sonograms, no belly shots. No grand announcements. Most people didn't know we were expecting. Unless you were in our current life rotation, passing us by in the neighborhood, through homeschooling or work, you didn't know. Because we couldn't talk about something we weren't sure was really happening.

I think I wanted a do over.

On my next birthday, I'll be forty-eight. It was only a few weeks ago when I had a life-shifting thought that rocked my world. I was at the skating rink with Ila when I saw a parent come in with a baby. She climbed the steps to the seating area after dropping off her skater and came to join the other parents. The months-old baby was in a sling. Tender, soft, and new. The woman, flushed with life and the busyness of motherhood, glowed. Sweet right? Negative. My first thought? "Not feeling that stage again!" After decades of longing, I no longer wanted another baby. It's weird having those thoughts.

I confessed this to my husband who practically celebrated. Happy to have me off the baby track, he congratulated me for finally coming to my senses. I'm grateful to him for not laughing at me a few months after Ade' was born. He humored me but was always honest in sharing his position. He was done. We'd received our miracles and won the lottery after risking my life. That chapter of our lives for him, was over.

So I'm dancing toward an end to this journey. My body is quieting. I sense subtle changes in my cycle and in myself that signal the arrival of a new phase of life. I'm not sad. I will gracefully let go of the things of youth and embrace this next chapter.

I'm putting away dreams of fertility, birth, and babies. I can't complain. My motherhood career has been rich in ways I am grateful for. On the flip side of my grief, I found gratitude. I've known tears and surrender and redemption, and grace. I have many years of motherhood before me, and like I always say, "I'm still on the playground."

"Middle age is not the period of high anxiety that we've been led to believe. For most people, mid-life is the place to be." - **Patricia Cohen author of In Our Prime**

The Prayer...

Lord, I'm in transition, mid-life motherhood and a whole bunch of maybes. Calm the questions; provide direction. I'll listen when you call. Thank you for a graceful glide through the wonder of change. This time is different. Shaped by your truth, I'm wiser. And I trust you completely. Amen.

For Reflection...

Birth rates for women over age thirty-five have doubled in the past forty years. This can be attributed largely due to advances in reproductive medicine. Have you considered the possibility of mid-life motherhood?

Menopause may feel like it's somewhere out in the horizon, but it's part of your reproductive story. Take some time to think about what this kind of change might look like.

Day Off: Celebrating Transitions

A thought...

You can play a powerful role in the lives of the little ladies in your world. Take some time to pray for their reproductive futures. Pray their bodies operate in the perfection for which they were created. Pray for their cycles - that they be smooth and stress free. Pray for a beautifully made transition.

A few thoughts and a celebration of transition...

> *Last night, my first-born daughter joined me under the moonlight.*
> *We danced.*
> *She ... taking her first steps*
> *Pointing her toes in a warm pool of lunar loveliness*
> *Testing her connection with women, with wisdom ... and the beautifully made divine.*

> *Rumblings and quakes foretold the coming of this day.*

> *She moved and spun around me all year. We fought. Our cosmic collisions inevitable.*

> *Pulling away but still attracted, still attached to her center.*

> *My core. The Son.*

> *She stays on my radar.*
> *Orbiting around my mother sun*
> *We're establishing a new way of being.*

Mother / daughter, women? Stars?
Redefining our connection
Because she isn't a baby.
Anymore.
She was born a fierce woman of God
A supernova
And I will trail her brilliance
and give her reasons to track mine

She ... my girl, my lovely one, my pretty princess.
Shines bright.
There is another woman in the house.
Another beautifully made, creative and powerful – woman..

When You Think Infertility is Forever: Tell Your Story

I didn't want to be infertile forever. I thought talking about it after I'd gone through it would keep me trapped, contained in a world of desperate, unfulfilled dreams even though mine had come true. Because the word infertility, the feeling of it, has a way of coloring everything you do. Being infertile can make you bitter and cynical. And there's no hope or happiness for the infertile. Right? Part of the trap is you really believe the lies. You keep your <u>story</u> to yourself. But the truth is, writing about it and believing with other women has freed me.

Last week a friend said to me, "Lisha, you aren't infertile anymore." And I jumped back. Inside anyway. I'm pretty cool on the exterior and can hold that kind of thing in. Anyway, it struck something deep in me. I'm not infertile. Saying that makes me cry. Because I've never said it. The weight of those words tell a long-ago tale of a girl who wanted to be a mama but wasn't. They weigh heavily on my soul because that girl was me.

That girl is me. I am not infertile, but I remember, in a good way.

Adoption doesn't cure infertility, but becoming a mother healed me. Baptism into the mother - hood by any means necessary was what I needed. Being a mother numbed me to the word infertility. The word, the fact was real. But God's truth transforms, and I no longer felt defeated by it. My daily life wasn't consumed by it.

I wondered if writing, engaging in dialogue, asking questions, and praying about all this was perhaps a trick to keep me from moving forward. Can I write about infertility forever? Will I identify with infertility forever?

Yes. And no.

Yes. I will identify with infertility forever. God keeps my heart soft for the current warriors in battle. I know my story, encouragement, and prayer are God's calling on my life to use something broken ... my redeemed journey, for His glory.

No. I don't expect I'll write solely about infertility forever. I am a multi-faceted woman with opinions and beliefs I want to share. I have stories to tell. I am alive and strive to be authentic. I can't do that if I only talk about infertility. I can't do that if I hold back from telling the other stories. Infertility is part of my story, but it isn't the whole story. I know He has other secrets to share with me, other mysteries he'll reveal. I'll write about those as they come. The profound lessons learned on this path transfer to just about any hardship in life. I can easily see them woven into the fabric of adventures to come.

I did have a baby. And after so many years of infertility, it was weird. And hard. I felt like a traitor. I had to come to terms with that. Dual citizenship has its benefits, but I thought someday I'd have to choose: have the baby and walk away into the supposed sunset in the land of the fertile? Or stay, available for service to others? My instinct was always to reach back ... at least try to help. I never considered walking away. I chose to tell the story.

I don't want to down-play the miracle. God showed up big in my life. But I know His purpose, His plan in me was hard-won. And it was won through my infertility. I can't forget that. He used that season to seal me. Am I infertile forever? No. The word infertility doesn't define me, but it has shaped part of my calling.

I am a warrior for women, and most importantly, I am forever His. My story is interlaced with the forever of his eternal love.

The Word...

"I will declare that your love stands firm forever, that you have established your faithfulness in heaven itself." **(Psalm 89:2)**

The Prayer...

Lord, use me. Use my experience, my life, for your glory. Help me tell the stories, the lessons you lovingly taught me when I didn't want to hear. The ones you walked me through. Especially the ones I stumbled through. Help me tell the stories you used to shape the person I am today. The stories belong to you. Use me to tell them. Lord, let me tell your story. Amen.

For Reflection...

What say you? Do you feel defined by infertility? What have you learned? Have you considered telling your story - from the right now of your journey? How can you channel the experience to positively affect others? Yourself?

How to Thrive

Do you want to thrive?

In the process, we find God's promise. It is a story of redemption and grace. God uses our struggles to draw us to Himself. He reveals a greater sense of his love. We walk away from the battle with wisdom from the journey poured on us like oil, our very being saturated in a love-soaked garment of praise. You just don't make it through the battle without a greater sense of his love, a clearer understanding of how this life is all about the process. The promise is the fulfillment of his purpose in you. It's there we begin to thrive.

How do we thrive when faced with infertility? What does it look like? I gathered a list of infertility warriors who are doing just that. Most are women like you, in the throes of battle. They fight bravely in the *now* of their infertility. Some have resolved their infertility by becoming parents; still others have chosen to fight the battle publicly through advocacy. All share vital, redemptive, life-changing words. They tell their stories.

This is what it means to thrive.

First a resource ...

Fertile Thoughts - Before there were blogs, I began online friendships and connections at Fertile Thoughts. Some of the relationships continue today, over twelve years later. I found the site as a new adoptive parent and would go online to ask questions about my new mama struggles. I was concerned with attachment and had questions about adoptive nursing. I connected with women who understood me, women who

100

wanted/ needed to express their feelings and share their stories in a community of women like them. There is nothing like connecting with your tribe to make any hardships you face doable. I loved the community there, and even though we've never met, I consider Jamie Doffing, my friend forever.

I'm loving Fertility for Colored Girls and its founder **Rev. Stacey L. Edwards-Dunn.**

Many want to know, why a separate organization for women of color?

Here's an answer from the site:

Research shows that among the 7.3 million women/couples in the United States, approximately 11.5 percent of African American women compared to 7 percent of white women experience a variety of infertility problems.

Unfortunately, even though these alarming rates of infertility among African-American women exist, studies show and Dr. Désirée McCarthy-Keith, a reproductive endocrinologist at Georgia Reproductive Specialists states that women of color utilize fertility services less often and seek medical care too late.

There are many reasons why African-American women fail to seek infertility care. The following are a few examples:

- Cost of Infertility Services
- Access to Infertility Services
- Lack of Education and Awareness
- Shame and Fear
- Lack of Health Care
- Lack of Support
- Lack of Finances
- Culture
- Limited Awareness of Treatment Options

- Lack of Access to Treatment Options

This is a good God thing. Organizations like Fertility for Colored Girls offer a safe place for women of color to share their stories. Awareness, advocacy, and education is essential to combating the issue of infertility among African-American Women.

And a few others that inspire me (in no particular order)

Natasha Metzler - The beautiful writing on this blog drew me in. Now I'm a cheerleader for Natasha. She is the author of *Pain Redeemed* and the mother of a beautiful young girl through adoption.

The Broken Brown Egg – This is another organization that speaks to the needs of women of color. This site features straight talk and a lot of humor about infertility. Regina Townsend brings the goods on infertility awareness using her real life journey.

Wanza Lefwich All faith. All the time. With Wanza you have to believe. Wanza is the author of *Faith and Fertility* and was one of my first twitter friends. She is also a motivational speaker and business builder.

A Royal Daughter - This is a beautiful Christian lifestyle blog of an infertility warrior. Amanda gave birth to a healthy baby boy last year. Yay!

Jennifer Kostick - Jennifer keeps me on my toes in the blogosphere. She beautifully represents Christ through a story of redemption after loss. You can get a free copy of her e-book Mercy Waits on her blog.

Marcy Hanson - Foster care advocate, adoptive mama and full-time nurse, Marcy is on it. Marcy is the author of *No Maybe*

Baby and the online hostess at the blog www.marcynellhanson.com.

Stay tuned for The HeartSpa , a new blog coming soon by **Resealia McKinney**, my (In)couragers community group co-leader at THRIVE (in)fertility.

And the blog of infertility warrior **Hysha Robinson** *Mrs. New York America 2013*. Using her personal struggles with infertility as a platform, Hysha won the crown.

The Word…

> *"The righteous shall flourish like a palm tree,*
> *He shall grow like a cedar in Lebanon.*
> *Those who are planted in the house of the Lord*
> *Shall flourish in the courts of our God.*
> *They shall still bear fruit in old age;*
> *They shall be fresh and flourishing,*
> *To declare that the Lord is upright;*

> *He is my rock, and there is no unrighteousness in Him."*- **(Psalm 92: 12-15)**

Inspiration…

"My mission in life is not merely to survive, but to thrive; and to do so with some passion, some compassion, some humor, and some style" - **Maya Angelou**

"Surviving is important. Thriving is elegant." - **Maya Angelou**

"We all have within us the ability to move from struggle to grace." - Arianna Huffington

The Prayer...

Lord, I'm walking in your perfect plan. I'm pushing past anything negative, grabbing hold of your grace. I won't let go. I want more from life. I choose to thrive. Give me the gift of your words - divine revelation singing peace to my soul. Let your wisdom-soaked truth come alive in me. Lord I want more. I choose to thrive. Amen.

Warrior Song

This armor is heavy, it presses on my shoulders and weighs me down. It's heavy and I can't lift my arms. Barely swinging in time with my stride, they slow my pace. I'm fighting a battle with an enemy I didn't expect. I'm tired.

What will winning look like? What will put an end to this war? I stab blindly into the dark abyss of infertility. My sword, twisted and bent from use. My jabs, barely enough to keep my enemy at bay. Most days I don't even try. It's a wonder this has gone on so long. How am I fighting this battle alone?

Friends creep towards the front lines to whisper words of hope. But they don't stay long. She breathes fear and loneliness. The dragon of infertility leaves even the bravest silent. The bloody battles of menstruation, miscarriage and loss, so formidable - we dare not speak their names. Friends...run away.

I pull a thread bare cloak around me to keep warm and push through an endless patch of dried leaves. I barely lift my feet. I need to feel connected. Grounded. Bound forever to something bigger than myself.

And I hear it. The small cries of a woman in the distance. I've come to know this muffled sound well. The new warriors don't like to cry. They never want to cry. But I'm here to welcome her, baptize her in the ring of fire. I'm here to stop the bleeding, bind the wounds, and help her recover from a loss that cuts wide and deep. She doesn't know it, but she'll play savior to my soul as well. Our tears mingling in a river of grief turned praise. Her presence assures my purpose, and in community we'll find strength. Together, we'll heal.

I turn, taking steps toward the sound, and then ... remember. God is here in this empty place. In this place of dry bones - where the sun won't shine, He does. And I feel it. I feel Him. I don't, we don't - fight alone.

And then, the lullaby of love stuck in the pit of my heart springs forth. And I open my mouth wide to sing.

> *This is the warrior song.*
> *I hear it.*
> *Piercing the barrier, breaking the veil*
> *Renewing faith and finding strength*
> *A voice rising and falling ... the ebb and flow of the warrior's*
> *cry*
> *Pick up your sword*
> *Warrior strong, warrior long*
> *He battles with you.*
> *So sprinkle notes of hope*
> *Sing a song of love and praise*
> *This is the warrior song, and I'll sing it loud and true.*
> *I'll sing it over you.*

The Word...

"He said, Hearken, all Judah, you inhabitants of Jerusalem, and you King Jehoshaphat. The Lord says this to you: Be not afraid or dismayed at this great multitude; for the battle is not yours, but God's." **(2 Chronicles 20:15 AMP)**

The Prayer...

Lord, the battle is yours. I fight, but only in your name. Give me strength to conquer any challenge, defeat any foe. Because I believe in you, I won't succumb to fear. Equip me to love as you do - unconditionally. When I'm weak, breathe life into the dry bones of my faith. I want to see and be seen by you. Amen.

National Infertility Awareness Week

Not only is your story worth telling, but it can be told in words so painstakingly eloquent that it becomes a song. – **Gloria Naylor**

Life is a moving breathing thing. We have to be willing to constantly evolve. Perfection is constant transformation. – **Nia Peeples**

I used to chide myself for not telling my story sooner. A year ago, I watched online – open jawed, as women bravely told their stories of infertility – mid-battle. They bore unimaginable pain and loss…unsuccessful treatments … publicly - in real time and in, the moment. I thought I'd failed. I realize now every story, even the story told after the battle is important. Stories told, whether from the trenches or after the Medal of Honor is pinned, are equally valuable.

There are things you just won't know until it's over. That's the perspective I speak from, the voice God graced me with. I tell the story as a veteran. And as such, see the complete picture, things I couldn't see in the middle.

Here's a revelation. The body I have now is not the one I began the journey with. Each season marking the completion of a cycle, one broken rotation after another as my body fought to keep up…hit that 360 degrees. I'll very likely walk many more cycles before my time on earth is up. But I'd say I'm learning the fine art of shape shifting. I'll transition more easily next time around. Ooze like fiery lava as God pours the next mold.

I see my body then, my body now. From surgeries and losses to a split wide Red Sea miracle birth…I soul-wept from one form to another. I took the journey and now enjoy the peace of a pressed flower between the pages of a long shelved book.

Everything's quiet now but I couldn't have told the story in my first body. My current physical state knows both worlds. Living the before and after I see now how my body danced in the spirit realm while the devil watched. A soul battle of "epic proportions", my new teen would say. A physical death would have been the least of my worries…I needed the win so that my spirit might live.

I couldn't have told this story with perky breasts and an unmarred belly. Apparently before telling the story I'd need a few gray hairs and a little mild back pain. My body would demand respect. Devotion. Love. That's what happened, physically, as weeks turned months, turned years. Equal parts breaking down and building up. Healing happened in stages. My body needed time.

I had to be branded first…by holy hot words singed as truth on my soul. I couldn't write the words without tears.

I had to be branded first.

And in this ceremony … this sacred sacrament… scattered pieces of my soul marked mines. I skipped over sections, tried to avoid the many unrecognizable parts of my whole

That I'd be blown away was inevitable. Christ's love explosion strewn as a million stars across the sky – So that I might look up and see one… Him…in my darkness.

This is my warrior song. Hand scratched notes of hope engraved on the stone table of His glory. Blood soaked and redeemed…I return to the battlefield with these words…for you.

National Infertility Awareness Week is acknowledged annually on the weekend before Mothers' Day. In solidarity, I form a circle on my blog by passing the talking stick. Join me as I open my online space for fellow warriors to tell their stories. For the redemptive power of telling to light a fire, to free a soul.

There's space for you. Send me your words. Send me your story.
*

* submit posts to lisha.epperson@gmail.com * anonymous submissions welcome.

*Thank you for reading and sharing **The Process, The Promise: A journal for infertility prayer**. A free download of Warrior Song: notes of hope on infertility and adoption is available for subscribers to my blog.*

Acknowledgements

Hello Warriors,

Thank you family and friends

A blogging journey is nothing without community …

A special shout out to Martha Grimm Brady, Joanne Viola, Heather Mertens and Marcy Hanson: my 2013 top commenters. Tanya Jones, Dana Rainey, Chelle Wilson, Donna Walker-Kuhne and Nisaa Christie for being my people, the ones I can freely bounce ideas off.

To Deidra Riggs, Jennifer Dukes Lee, Michelle DeRusha, Diane Bailey, Shelly Miller, Susan Rinehart Stilwell, Mary Goodwin Bonner, and any other women who passed through the hotel room at Allume in October 2013. You changed my world by letting me into yours.

A special shout out to Dawn Hewitt for her listening ear, a nudge when I need it and encouragement to keep trying. And to Christal Jenkins for letting me know it's okay to press pause.

This work is the beginning of a love letter to Big Daddy and the Lovelies. I'll never stop writing it.

If you like this piece of work and want to stay connected subscribe to the blog at www.lishaepperson.com

Cover image Flickr CC – Andrej Villa

If you love it, help me share it by passing on the link for purchase to your friends.

If you mention the book on Facebook, Twitter, or Pinterest, please be sure to link back to www.lishaepperson.com

About the Author

Lisha Epperson is a hopeful romantic, lover of Jesus and most things antique. A happy wife and now mother of five, she shares a warrior song about her fourteen year walk through infertility and the semi-sweet miracle of adoption. **Lisha** works out a life of faith with fear, trembling, and a fair measure of grace in New York City. Follow her blog at **www.lishaepperson.com**.

Made in the USA
Middletown, DE
30 December 2022

20739881R00073